Josephine Fairley is the Beauty Editor of the *Mail On Sunday*'s *YOU Magazine*, and the co-author, with Sarah Stacey, of the bestselling *The Beauty Bible*. She has written on the subject of beauty and health for a wide range of magazines including *Marie Claire*, *Health & Beauty*, *Woman's Journal*, *Harpers & Queen*, *The Clothes Show Magazine*, *Woman & Home*, *Cleo*, *Mode* and the *Sydney Morning Herald*. She is also a winner of the Jasmine Award, the fragrance industry's top literary award. In her early twenties, she was Britain's youngest-ever magazine editor, editing first *Look Now* and then *Honey*.

Josephine Fairley describes herself as 'a fragranceaholic' and has possibly the largest bathroom cabinet in West London.

Also available in Orion paperback

HEALTH SPA AT HOME

JOSEPHINE FAIRLEY

ORION

An Orion Paperback
First published in Great Britain in 1998 by
Orion Books Ltd,
Orion House, 5 Upper St Martin's Lane,
London WC2H 9EA

A CIP catalogue record for this book
is available from the British Library.

ISBN: 0 75281 545 8

Printed and bound in Great Britain by
The Guernsey Press Co. Ltd, Guernsey

CONTENTS

INTRODUCTION

One day, I'm convinced, scientists are going to discover that simply *saying* the word 'spa' reduces blood pressure, melts away stress, maybe even saves our sanity. The thought of escaping, of stopping the world and getting off for a few days of unashamed pampering, is a busy person's dream. The problem is, it's hard to find the time – and the money – for a spa escape. At the end of a rejuvenating day at a spa, your skin glows, your hair shines, your mind's at peace, and you're ready for anything – except the hefty bill! (There goes peace of mind...) And, in reality, juggling your life to make a window in the diary for a getaway – whether to a metropolitan 'day spa' or a pampering retreat in the wilderness – can create more angst than it dispels.

So the perfect solution is to create your own spa, at home. Health spa days at home – or, better still, a spa weekend like this – offer a heaven-sent opportunity to clear body and

> *The perfect solution is to create your own spa, at home*

mind. With the high-quality natural bath and beauty products available today – many of them to be found as close as the shelf in your nearest health food store – you can recreate the effect of visiting a hot mineral spring, having an aromatherapy treatment or a facial, without leaving your own bathroom.

This simple 48-hour programme telescopes many of the body-and-soul restoring effects of a stay at a spa into just two days. It introduces you to techniques and therapies which can – if enjoyed regularly – help you stay on top of stress and fatigue. What's more, it lets you enjoy being at Home, Sweet Home without any of the usual responsibilities or chores. Take the opportunity to ban housework. Disconnect the TV, so that the outside world can't intrude on your private paradise. Take a break from the hustle and rustle of newspapers, filled with their bad news and scandal. Take the phone off the hook, or switch on the answering machine, if you have one: it's hard to muster the discipline *not* to leap up and answer the phone when it rings. (As it surely will, the second you dip your big toe in the bath.) If you have young children, get your partner to take them away to their grandparents or to a favourite aunt for the weekend – because it's impossible to get the full benefits of the health spa at home if you have children clamouring for your attention. Don't think of this as selfishness. We all have so many demands on our time and energies from other people that we need all the personal strength and energy we can muster. Creating a health spa at home is a way of restoring that balance so that we can stay on top of all life's demands.

Of course, the health spa at home can be a private retreat from the world – or you can invite your friends and/or partner, a daughter or your mother, to share it. It's a wonderful idea for a pampering 'hen party', too. When I was writing this book, a group of girl-friends and I took time out to create a mini-health farm, at home,

> *A wonderful idea for a pampering 'hen party'*

with four of us taking turns to perform treatments – and be treated. (Which gave us real 'quality' time together, as opposed to trying to catch up over a rushed cappuccino, or on the phone with children squealing in the background.)

But whether you retreat into this spa world alone or with companions, the key is to indulge, indulge, indulge. After just 48 hours, you will emerge refreshed, revived, even rejuvenated, with the knots soaked from your spine – and your soul. (You'll be polished to perfection, too – from squeaky-clean top to cuticle-free toe.) And, unlike a trip to a genuine spa, you won't find your baggage has been re-routed to Istanbul, or that your car has picked up a parking ticket. In fact, the anxieties that so preoccupied you before your mind-and-body treat will have evaporated with the essential oils or been sluiced down the plug-hole.

So enjoy …

Never feel guilty spending time on pure self-focus. According to psychologist Dr Cary Cooper, among others, setting aside time for yourself can enhance not only your appearance but your overall wellbeing. 'Simple, sensual acts such as touching and bathing can improve self-esteem, as well as reducing anxiety,' he says.

CHAPTER ONE

Shopping for your Spa Weekend

A little homework – and preparation – will make all the difference to your 48 hours. The programme runs from Friday evening to Sunday evening, but reading through the book once before you embark on the programme will give you an idea of exactly what the spa programme entails – and let you plan around your personal preferences. This will not only save you spending money on items you won't be needing, but it's decidedly unrelaxing to keep dashing to the shops for more cotton wool, or have the washing machine distract from your meditation as you try to keep up with the demand for towels. In fact, many of the essentials you'll already have – in your store cupboard and your linen cupboard …

YOUR HEALTH SPA SHOPPING LIST

- Batteries for your CD/cassette player. (You'll be listening to music in the bathroom, where it's dangerous to have your stereo hooked up to a live electrical supply.) Make a pile of all the cassettes and CDs you think you might like to listen to. (New Age tapes – of nature sounds, in particular – and classical music are most conducive to unwinding)

- Plenty of purified water. If you don't want to buy bottled mineral water, invest in a filter jug (at good pharmacies), which will remove many of the impurities. You are aiming to de-tox over the weekend, and unfiltered tap water is anything but pure
- A pile of the fluffiest towels you can muster, and a towelling bath robe, if you have one
- A book of poetry or short stories. (Nothing that will grip you so much that you can't bear to put it down for your pedicure. And besides, if you take the juice fasting option, your concentration may not be as good as usual)
- Paper handkerchiefs
- A journal/diary for writing in
- A few pretty postcards, or art cards
- Scented candles/aromatherapy burner (for use with your essential oils)
- Clingfilm and a 'space blanket' from a mountaineering/ hiking store
- Large pillows (preferably the foam kind, used on outdoor furniture – or sofa cushions; and make sure you have enough towels to cover them)
- A rolling pin (or a 'footsie' roller)
- Pumice stone and/or foot file
- Natural bristle body brush/loofah or scrub mitt/flannel/agave cloth/sponge
- If you're going to treat yourself to a manicure/pedicure, you'll need a hoof stick, orange sticks, nail varnish remover, base coat, top coat and the coloured nail polish of your choice, plus toe dividers, if you like to use them
- Fresh fruit and vegetables (organic where possible) – see The Big Squeeze, page 10 and Heavenly Wholefoods, page 15, to help you prepare a more detailed grocery list.

For Heavenly Wholefoods, you'll also need seaweed
(or kelp tablets), from your health food store, miso soup,
rice cakes, psyllium seeds and sunflower seeds

- Honey
- Milk or milk powder (for bathing!)
- 1 kg (about 2 lb) rough sea salt
- 6 free-range eggs
- Apple cider vinegar
- Dried rosemary leaves
- Oatmeal/cornmeal
- Cucumber, potatoes, tea bags, fresh figs or witch hazel
  (for your 'eye brightener', page 38)
- Herbal teas (see page 107 for suggestions)
- Essential oils (see Aquacadabra, page 40, and Breathe
  Deeply, page 65, for suggestions, but a basic, useful essen-
  tial oils kit could include lavender, tea tree, rosemary and
  geranium. See page 30 for details of how to do a patch
  test, which you should do the night before your health
  spa, if you haven't used these essential oils before)
- Soapwort herb (if you want to make the Ultra-Gentle
  Shampoo, see Hair Treats, pages 76 to 78)
- Seaweed mask (home-made or store-bought – optional,
  see Marine Magic, page 118)
- Clay/mud treatments (optional, see Wallow in Mud, page 122)

CHAPTER TWO

Food for Body and Soul

T he food at spa retreats is specifically designed to nourish the body and the soul – and at the same time, to help you de-tox. You will be eating pure, natural foods over the weekend – and you have the option of a juice 'mini-fast', or a diet that focuses on wholefoods. The choice is yours …

THE BIG SQUEEZE: JUICE FAST

If you want to lose a pound or two, or feel you've overloaded your body with junk lately, you can combine your pampering with a juice fast. You'll replace some or all of your usual meals with a combination of delicious fresh-squeezed fruit and vegetable juices. Fans of juicing believe that it can, variously, clear the mind (and the complexion), peel off pounds, send energy levels soaring, put the sparkle back in your eyes, defeat constipation and even blitz hangovers. What they *don't* always mention is that juice fasting may, temporarily, make you feel tired and lethargic, and will probably make your breath smell – signs that the toxins are being eliminated from your system …

That might not sound too attractive – and it's why the juicing element of your spa weekend is entirely optional – but juice fasting does offer distinct benefits. By Sunday evening, any light-headedness should

Before juicing to clear your mind and body, you definitely need to clear your diary

have passed and you should feel boundlessly energetic and ready to face the week ahead. The perfect time to enjoy a juice fast, in fact, is a weekend off; before juicing to clear your mind and body, you definitely need to clear your diary. (And summer is a better time than winter: our bodies require less food in the warm months than when the wind's whistling and it's freezing out there.)

Devotees of juicing believe that raw juice is the most perfect fuel for your body. The high water content of fruit means that it's easily assimilated by the body and tends to cleanse and nurture it, while supplying it with a full range of essential nutrients. The idea of juice fasting is that the body is best able to heal itself of whatever ails it when the system – particularly the digestive system – is given a rest. Juicing fans also swear that fasting this way swiftly 'purifies' the body, ridding it of the potentially harmful build-up of toxins (such as agrochemicals and other pollutants, which may linger in the digestive system). But unlike most fasts, by drinking juices, you're getting your full quota of nutrients.

Most of us, of course, could boast of having a carton of juice in the fridge. But pre-packed juices simply don't offer all the health-and-beauty benefits of the whizz-it-yourself variety; ready-made juices rely on concentrated juice and extra water to bulk them up. Look on the label and you'll find that some juices contain additives such as sugar, colours, flavours and preservatives, too, and they've often been pasteurised. Fresh-squeezed juices are as nature intended.

For your weekend spa fast, then, you need to get in a generous supply of fresh fruits and vegetables.

The endless fruit 'n' veg permutations guarantee against boredom. No two juices need be the same – the only limit is your imagination, so be adventurous. Beetroot juice, cabbage juice – even potato juice – can be delicious. Sprouted pulses – for instance, alfalfa or chickpeas – and seeds (such as pumpkin and sun-flower seeds) can be whizzed in the blender, too. Drink fruit *and* vegetable juices, to get the maximum nutritional benefit; drinking too many

> *Drink fruit and vegetable juices, to get the maximum nutritional benefit*

fruit juices leads to a build-up of acidity (and may trigger spots and breakouts). Do make a point of seeking out organic fruit and vegetables, however, whenever possible. Blackcurrants, for example, may have been sprayed up to eleven times before they reach the supermarket shelf, so if you juice your fruit and veggies, you're juicing pesticides, too. If you can't find organic produce, wash your fruit and vegetables in water to which a couple of drops of environmentally friendly washing-up liquid have been added. Then rinse.

The secret to not feeling deprived is to look upon each glass of juice as a meal in itself. It's quite simple: if you swallow a pint of juice in a couple of seconds, you're going to feel starving – even if that's just psychological. Sip, slowly – that way, the enzymes in your saliva start to break it down before the juice hits the stomach, too. To begin with, beginners should start with up to three 225 ml/8 fl oz glasses of juice a day. You should also drink plenty of water, herbal teas and/or grain coffee substitutes between juice 'meals', to keep well-hydrated. It's an idea to dilute dark green vegetables – such as broccoli, spinach, watercress – and dark red veggies (like red cabbage and beetroot), with pure water, four parts to one.

You don't really need a special juicer to make juice drinks. If you have a blender, simply put the whole (or peeled) fruits and vegetables in there, and whizz. You'll get a thicker juice –

but it'll be more meal-like. And one last word of juice advice: drink as soon as possible after juicing, as fresh juices quickly lose their vitamins and minerals. Here are suggestions for some fabulous juice concoctions. Once you've got the idea, you can experiment with your own recipes. Let your taste buds be your guide!

> **WARNING** Because fruit juice causes a rapid rise in blood sugar, anyone suffering from candidiasis, low blood sugar or diabetes should take professional advice before upping their intake of fresh juices; a juice fast may not be suitable for you.

GINGER ZINGER

- 2 apples
- 2 oranges
- 2 cm (3/4 in) cube of fresh ginger

This simple, tangy drink is quick and easy to prepare. Wash and slice the apples, peel the ginger, peel the oranges, leaving the pith – then juice and enjoy!

GREEN POWER JUICE

- 1/4 head of green cabbage
- 2 apples
- 1 celery stick

This green 'mega juice' has a pungent flavour and is an excellent way to drink your greens. Wash the ingredients, slice the apples, trim the celery, then juice.

SKIN-IMPROVER JUICE
....

- 1/4 red (bell) pepper
- 1/4 green (bell) pepper
- 1/3 large cucumber

Juice each ingredient separately, then blend using a spoon.
(To keep skin clear of blemishes, well-toned and healthy, you
need juices like these that are high in vitamins C, E and
beta-carotene, the minerals zinc and potassium, and which
stimulate the digestive system and kidneys to work efficiently.)

ENERGY V-R-O-O-O-M
....

- 1 mango
- 1/2 medium pineapple
- 1 banana, mashed
- 150 ml (1/4 pint) milk or 1 small pot plain yoghurt
- 1 teaspoon desiccated coconut
- 1/2 teaspoon honey

Juice each fruit, then blend in the other ingredients with a
spoon, for an instant pick-you-up.

TAKE-IT-EASY JUICE
....

- 1 large green apple, whole
- 2 celery sticks
- 8–10 lettuce leaves

Juice, and drink before bedtime, or when you are feeling
particularly tense.

APPLE AND SPINACH
....

- 3 whole apples
- A handful of spinach

Juice, and drink twice a day. It's especially good before bedtime; the combination of apple and spinach is extremely effective for cleansing the digestive tract and improving elimination quickly.

HEAVENLY WHOLEFOODS: 48 HOUR DE-TOX DIET

If you don't want to embark on a juice regime, make whole-foods the focus of your meals, wherever possible. If you're serious about following this no-fat, sugar-free diet for a couple of days, but you're worried your resolve will crack – then clear out the fridge of items that might tempt you. (You can always store them in a friend's fridge till Monday.) If you're a die-hard snacker, place bowls of organic fresh fruit around the house. Then at least if you're tempted, you'll be *healthily* tempted.

Life is toxic. You'd have to live in a baby Biosphere, breathing purified oxygen and eating only organic foods, for it to be anything else. As a result, the urge to purge occasionally grips most of us – to clear our systems of 'lifestyle debris': filthy air, processed foods, that bottle of cheap wine bar plonk that you mistakenly drank the other day, and which now seems to be poisoning your entire system. Even our own bodies and the bacteria in our intestines produce toxins. As Dr Dwight McKee, Medical Director of the International Health Institute in America, succinctly puts it, 'Anybody who has lived the mainstream Western lifestyle for ten or more years has seventy trillion garbage cans for cells.'

What is a toxin? According to experts, a toxin is anything foreign to the body that impairs its natural functioning – such as pollution, nicotine, alcohol – and can cause damage if not eliminated. (Even stress can be toxic, by causing hormonal imbalances – or simply driving you to abuse toxic substances.) Usually, you get rid of toxins when you sweat, urinate or breathe. But if the body is exposed to a higher toxic level than it can handle, sooner or later you'll feel the effects. (What happens, for example when you have a hangover, is that the body has taken in too much alcohol and its ability to process the chemical waste is impaired.)

> 'Anybody who has lived the mainstream Western lifestyle for ten or more years has seventy trillion garbage cans for cells'

In fact, it's been observed by some health experts that a person's health is mainly determined by the ability of their body to de-toxify. So de-toxification isn't something that should be restricted to the Elizabeth Taylors and the Betty Fords of this world. Every now and then we should all give our systems a break, to get rid of the toxic substances that accumulate in the body and

> A *person's health is mainly determined by the ability of their body to* de-toxify

can, in many cases, be linked with specific diseases: carbon monoxide and cadmium with coronary heart disease, excessive fluoride with sight reduction, lead (from old piping) with stomach problems. Exposure to food additives, solvents, pesticides and herbicides can lead to everything from depression and headaches to increased cancer rates – not to mention cellulite, as the body builds up fatty pockets around chemicals it wasn't designed to cope with! The list is endless. And *scary*, as the by-products of modern living take their toll on our health. They get stored in the body and encourage not only degenerative diseases, but early ageing, too. Still, the *good* news is that de-toxification isn't difficult – and better still, it can incorporate body therapies and beauty treatments which pamper as they flush out all that unwanted junk. And your health spa weekend at home is the perfect place to start.

Juice fasting, as I've explained, is one way to de-tox. But it isn't practical for everyone; it can sap energy and make concentrating impossible. So you may prefer to base your food this weekend around a diet of Oriental-inspired wholefood recipes, instead.

> *De-toxification isn't difficult – and better still, it can incorporate body therapies and beauty treatments which pamper as they flush out all that unwanted junk*

At the end of a 48-hour regime, you'll find you have an extraordinary spring in your step, tangible clear-headedness and vitality. (Not to mention better skin, long-term – although you may find, in the first few days, that you suffer 'breakouts', as toxins rise to the surface of your body.) It also strengthens the resolve to stick to a purer lifestyle (until the next time wickedness beckons, at least!) The 48-hour De-tox Diet is high in fibre, aiming to clear these deposits and give more muscle tone to the large intestine. Apart from a splash for your delicious nightly stir-fry, cut out oil altogether: your body will start to draw on its own reserves if you don't eat oil, and *that's* when you start getting rid of those toxins.

This diet is the spring-clean almost *everyone's* system needs. It focuses on foods found to be particularly effective at banishing toxins from the body: beetroot, celery, fennel, white radish (now found in most supermarkets); they all contain natural diuretics that help remove excess fluid, which is why they're good for anyone prone to cellulite. Seaweed, meanwhile, is great for enhancing metabolism – but if you can't find seaweed, take kelp tablets. Water is vital: eight glasses a day help flush the wastes from your body more quickly, and 'fill you up'; you can also drink herbal teas or grain coffee substitutes, without milk. But in fact, there's absolutely no need to go hungry on this diet: you can always snack on rice cakes, or miso soup, or salad, if you get peckish. The 48-Hour De-tox Diet gives you all the nutrients your body requires. The only extras you'll need are capsules containing psyllium husks (to help spring-clean the intestines), and the occasional handful of sunflower seeds, which are high in pectin – a valuable source of fibre which also helps recover vital bile salts in the large intestine, helping the body to be *really* efficient.

> *This diet is the spring-clean almost everyone's system needs*

> *Water is vital: eight glasses a day help flush the wastes from your body*

Unlike some diets, this won't make you woozy with hunger – but still, try to schedule it for a time like this, when your diary isn't crowded. Although the diet will help you maintain a high energy level, for maximum benefits it's *vital* to avoid stress. (One downside of the diet may be occasional bad breath. But take that as your signal that the de-toxifying process has truly begun. It isn't just our digestive systems and kidneys that excrete toxins; so do our lungs.)

If you can't retreat to a Himalayan monastery to live on clear air, brown rice and pure thoughts, then de-toxify regularly at home. It sure beats living in a bubble!

- Eat slowly and carefully; really chew every mouthful.
- Try to get a daily dose of sunshine, to boost immunity – just 10 or 20 minutes a day will do.
- The diet should not be followed for more than 48 hours.
- If you suffer from high or low blood pressure, diabetes, kidney problems or usually follow a special diet, consult with your doctor before following this programme.

YOUR HEALTH SPA DE-TOX DIET

FRIDAY EVENING

Dinner
Brown rice and stir-fried vegetables
Grated white radish
2 psyllium seed capsules

SATURDAY

Breakfast
High-fibre muesli

Lunch
Miso soup and puffed rice cakes with beetroot and oil-free vinaigrette – or lemon juice. (Eat as many rice cakes as you like, making sure you chew well.)

Dinner
Brown rice and stir-fried vegetables
2 psyllium seed capsules

SUNDAY

Breakfast
High-fibre muesli
Lunch
Salad of white radish, fennel and frisée lettuce, with oil-free
vinaigrette or lemon juice
Dinner
Brown rice and stir-fried vegetables
Grated white radish
2 psyllium seed capsules

RECIPES

HIGH-FIBRE SUGAR-FREE MUESLI

- 175 g/6 oz oat flakes
- 2 tablespoons wheat bran
- 8 tablespoons raisins
- 4 tablespoons sunflower seeds
- 1 teaspoon grated peel from an organic, or well-scrubbed, orange
- 1/2 teaspoon grated peel from an organic, or well-scrubbed, lemon
- 1–2 apples, grated

The night before, combine all the ingredients except the apple,
and add enough filtered water to the mixture to make a thick
soup, erring on the side of too much rather than too little.
Next morning give it a good stir, and the oats will make it
creamy – even without milk. If it's too runny, add a bit more
of the muesli mixture. Grate apple into the muesli just before
eating. This recipe makes enough for two breakfasts.

BEETROOT SALAD

- 1 medium beetroot, peeled and grated
- 1 apple, grated
- 1 shallot or small onion, chopped
- 3 sprigs of parsley
- 2 tablespoons apple cider vinegar
- A pinch of salt

Combine all the ingredients well and eat straight away.

MISO SOUP

- 2 tablespoons miso (from health food stores)
- 450 ml/16 fl oz water
- Piece of wakame or other seaweed
- 4 tablespoons chopped vegetables, steamed or sautéed

Mix the miso with the water, add other ingredients and simmer gently for 10 minutes. (Alternatively, you can find instant miso soup in most good health food stores.)

PERFECT BROWN RICE

Always check your rice for foreign bodies: tiny stones or other particles can spoil the enjoyment of a meal. Then wash the rice by putting the saucepan of rice under a running tap and letting the water flow over the top. For each cupful of brown rice, add 1 3/4 cupfuls of water, and half a teaspoon of salt. (Use a cup that holds about 225 ml/8fl oz of liquid.) Bring the water to the boil and allow to boil for 3 minutes. Reduce the heat to the lowest possible level and simmer, covered, for 40 minutes to 1 hour, or until the water has all been absorbed and the rice is just beginning to scorch. Remove from the heat and allow to stand for 5 minutes. Do not stir rice while it's cooking.

To reheat the rice, place your serving in a metal sieve, with a plate covering it, and gently steam over a pan of simmering water. Allow about 5 minutes for the steam to warm it through. Be careful that the simmering water does not touch the rice – it will get soggy!

STIR-FRIED VEGETABLES
••

Here's where the variety really comes in. By changing the vegetables regularly, always using organic when available (don't *re-tox* while you de-tox!), you never get bored, despite eating a very simple diet. Avoid potatoes, tomatoes, aubergines and chilli peppers; these are excluded from a macrobiotic diet, on which this de-tox is based. Apart from these, you can use anything, even Brussels sprouts, but here are a few delicious combinations:

- Baby corn, beansprouts and peas
- Spring greens, celery and diced carrots
- Carrots, turnips and cabbage
- Peas, carrots and celery
- White radish, red radish and leeks
- Fennel bulbs, peas and chopped chicory heads

The stir-fry always starts with finely chopped onions and a few finely chopped cloves of garlic – pre-cook these with a splash of virgin olive oil in a wok or frying pan until they begin to turn golden and translucent. Meanwhile, cut all the other chosen vegetables into small strips or cubes so that the heat can penetrate all parts quickly. Add them to the pre-cooked onions and garlic, coat lightly in the oil and stir-fry at a high heat for a few minutes, taking care to turn the veggies so they all get the heat but none gets burned. Then add a little water at the bottom of the pan, sprinkle with a dash of soy sauce, season with a pinch of salt and cover – letting it steam for a few minutes until most of the juice has evaporated. Stir-fry vegetables should have a slightly *al dente* quality, just barely over the line from rawness.

For variations, try Japanese-style: use white radish in cubes, along with slices of shiitake mushroom and matchstick-sliced carrots; add a little mirin rice wine* with the soya sauce and water, and sprinkle the vegetables with green nori* seaweed flakes. (*From health food stores.) Or Thai-style: finely chop the inner stalks of lemon grass with peeled fresh ginger, and add to the oil with a bit of black pepper (or better still, green peppercorns) at the same time as the vegetables. Add fresh coriander leaves along with the water, at the steaming stage. For a herbal stir-fry, add chopped parsley, dill tops and other herbs of your choice to the vegetables at the steaming stage. Herbs go particularly well with vegetables such as spring greens, curly kale, leeks and fennel bulbs.

Serve with warmed brown rice.

THOUGHTS ON LIVING A TOXIN-FREE LIFE ...

Once you've de-toxed, it's less tempting to go back to a junk-food lifestyle again. So here are some guidelines for living a purer life, in future ...

- Eat only organic produce, as far as possible
- Drink bottled water, to avoid the chemicals present in tap water. (Claudia Schiffer never goes anywhere without her bottle of Evian!)
- Enjoy daily massage or skin-brushing – to help eliminate built-up toxins, and banish unwelcome stress
- Breathe deeply. Get out into the fresh air, away from roads or obvious pollution sources
- To maintain the benefits long-term, cut down on sugar – or, preferably, cut it out altogether

- Minimise your intake of animal products – dairy and meat
- Avoid prescription drugs unless you're in a life-threatening situation – yet *more* chemicals which end up getting stored in unwelcome places …

WATER WORKS

> **Drinking a lot of water can actually reduce fluid retention**

Most of us don't drink nearly enough water. Ask any supermodel her stay-gorgeous secret and she'll almost certainly answer: 'Two litres of water a day.' Coffee, tea and cola drinks just don't count – in fact, they act like diuretics, and make you become more dehydrated. Most spa centres emphasise water drinking as a vital part of their 'cure' – and, surprisingly, drinking a lot of water can actually *reduce* fluid retention (a cause of excess weight). This is because water is often retained by your body as it tries to swill out minerals and toxins.

The water that comes out of your tap can be hard or soft, and is chemically purified by chlorination. Fluoride is also added – to reduce tooth decay – and there may be residues of aluminium (aluminium sulphate is added, to settle out solid impurities). In addition, it may contain pesticide residues (from farming run-off), or other chemicals. And water is recycled, so basically, last night's bathwater may cook tomorrow's vegetables.

The sensible approach, then, is to drink bottled water – or at least water that's been filtered. Even using a simple, jug-style filter that you can buy in a pharmacy is better than glugging water that has come straight from the tap. (Try making tea with filtered water, and compare it with a cup made using *unfiltered* water. You'll see that the filtered cuppa doesn't have a tell-tale scum on the top. Not only that, but filtered water reduces scale and kettle fur, clears murkiness and discoloration and leaves your tea tasting of tea, rather than chlorine.) Experts advise that still, room-temperature water is most compatible with your body, but if you really find luke-warm water unpalatable, do at least make your ice cubes with filtered water, too.

During your spa weekend, get in the habit of drinking eight glasses of water, paced throughout the day. Your body will love you for it …

Label-speak

Natural mineral waters are untreated, with nothing added and nothing removed. They can be still or sparkling; some waters emerge bubbling naturally from springs, while others have extra carbon added to make them fizz more. No water is pure H_2O but some natural waters have a combination of minerals that make them delicious – and good for the body.

Any bottled spring water is likely to be better for you than what pours straight out of the tap – but some may suit you more than others. Most labels carry a listing of what's inside: calcium (Ca), magnesium (Mg), potassium (K), sodium (Na), sulphates (SO_4), chlorides (Cl), nitrates (NO_3), fluoride (F), bicarbonates (HCO_3), plus the acid/alkaline balance. Quantities are usually listed in milligrams (mg) per litre (l), but may also be in milligrams per 100 millilitres (mg/100ml) or parts per million (ppm). Don't be confused: the bottom line is that you should look for reasonably high levels of calcium and magnesium – so they should be near the top of the list of minerals; they make the water 'hard' (and so good for your heart). Avoid high levels of sodium (bad for your blood pressure); keep levels of sulphates, chlorides, nitrates and fluorides low. The pH reading, meanwhile, signifies how acid the water is. Neutral is pH 7.0. Acidic water (low pH) will leach chemicals from water pipes and plastic bottles. A neutral or higher reading is therefore better.

CHAPTER THREE

Your 48-hour Spa Programme: Preview

At first glance, this schedule might sound action-packed – *not* what you need to unwind at all. But in fact, each of these therapies and activities has been specifically designed to unkink your muscles and unscramble your mind. Remember, though, there are no 'musts'; do as much or as little as you wish. Think of the week-end as a 'sampler', a smorgasbord of activities which you might like to try – and then incorporate into your 'real' life afterwards. (Or maybe just decide that they're not for you. The point is, until you've experienced juicing, yoga, aromatherapy, reflexology or whatever, you won't know if they're for you.)

FRIDAY EVENING
7.00 p.m. Juice Meal or Wholefood Dinner (see pages 10–23)
7.30 p.m. Frown-beating Massage
7.45 p.m. Make Your Feet Happy (reflexology and the ultimate pedicure)
8.30 p.m. Eye Brightener
9.00 p.m. Put Back the Glow (facial scrub)
9.15 p.m. Fragrance Meditation
9.30 p.m. Aquacadabra! (aromatherapy bath: body scrubbing and bathtime relaxation)
10.00 p.m. Mind/Body Journal
10.15 p.m. Bed

SATURDAY MORNING

7.30 a.m. Rise and Shine

8.00 a.m. Yoga ('Salute to the Sun' and other simple yoga movements)

9.00 a.m. Juice Meal or Wholefood Breakfast

9.15 a.m. Aromatherapy Hot Towel Facial

9.30 a.m. Body Splash

10.00 a.m. Breathe Deeply and Relax ... (meditation)

10.45 a.m. Walking Back to Happiness

11.45 a.m. Hair Treats (including scalp massage)

SATURDAY AFTERNOON

12.45 p.m. Juice Meal or Wholefood Lunch

1.15 p.m. Take A Break ...

1.35 p.m. Fabulous Facial

2.30 p.m. Clear the Air

3.00 p.m. Afternoon Walk

4.00 p.m. At-Home Waxing

5.00 p.m. Take A Break (or a nap...)

SATURDAY EVENING

7.00 p.m. Juice Meal or Wholefood Supper

7.30 p.m. Evening Meditation

8.00 p.m. Night-Time Milk Bath

9.00 p.m. Be Your Own Masseur (heavenly hand massage)

9.30 p.m. Loosen Your Tongue (relaxation exercise)

10.00 p.m. Mind/Body Journal

10.15 p.m. Sleep

SUNDAY MORNING

7.30 a.m. Rise and Shine

8.00 a.m. Yoga ('Salute to the Sun' and other simple yoga movements)

9.00 a.m. Juice Meal or Wholefood Breakfast

9.15. a.m. Aromatherapy Hot Towel Facial

10.00 a.m. Morning Walk

10.45 a.m. Learn How To Breathe ...

11.30 a.m. Herbal Teatime

11.45 a.m. Learn To Be Here Now ...

SUNDAY AFTERNOON

12 noon Juice Meal or Wholefood Lunch

1.00 p.m. Body Brushing Blitz

1.30 p.m. D-I-Y Hydrotherapy

2.00 p.m. Catch Up With Your Life

3.00 p.m. Get Fit – With a Twist (belly dancing!)

3.15 p.m. De-Junk Your Bathroom Cabinet (space-clearing)

4.00 p.m. Afternoon Walk

5.00 p.m. It's a Wrap (seaweed or mud wrap)

6.00 p.m. Five Simple Stretches

SUNDAY EVENING

6.30 p.m. Evening Meditation

7.00 p.m. Juice Meal or Wholefood Supper

8.00 p.m. D-I-Y Facial Massage

8.30 p.m. Aquacadabra (aromatherapy bath)

9.00 p.m. The Perfect 10 (manicure)

10.00 p.m. Mind/Body Journal

10.15 p.m. Sleep ...

THE NIGHT BEFORE ...

Essential oils – which you'll be using this weekend – are potent. In a few cases, they can trigger sensitivity, so it makes sense to try a **patch test** with the oils you may be using. The night before, wash and dry an area the size of a 10-pence piece on the inside of your forearm, and apply a drop of the essential oil, diluted with an equal part of vegetable oil. (Neat oils – except for lavender and tea tree – should never be applied to the skin.) Cover with a loose sticking plaster and wait for 24 hours. If you see any signs of irritation – such as redness or itching – avoid that particular oil. (If you're going to be using a blend of oils, do a patch test for each of them.)

Brown rice preparation
If you're going to be following the wholefood 48-Hour De-tox Diet, rather than the juicing programme, cook your brown rice now. (See page 21 for instructions on how to make perfect brown rice.)

CHAPTER FOUR

Friday Evening

7.00 P.M. JUICE MEAL OR WHOLEFOOD SUPPER

7.30 P.M. FROWN-BEATING MASSAGE

Stress makes us frown. Frowns, over time, make wrinkles. But, according to experts in facial exercise, giving your face a mini-workout can help beat habitual frowning – and the expression marks it leaves behind. (The face has around 45 muscles, and facial exercises can be performed to improve the tone of the whole face, or can be directed at specific problem areas – such as the forehead.) Top facial exercise expert Eva Fraser (see Resources) suggests the following workout to eliminate horizontal lines on the forehead.

1 Sit in front of a mirror, rest your elbows on a table and place the pads of your fingertips along your hairline.
2 Gently push your brow upwards and hold, keeping your head erect.
3 Looking straight ahead, bring your brow down in five movements against the resistance of your hands, and as you do so, gradually close your eyes.
4 Hold this downward pull for a count of three, then slowly release.
5 Don't scowl or push your head into your hands – it can cause tension in the back of your neck.
6 Relax and breathe.
7 Repeat three times.

7.45 P.M. MAKE YOUR FEET HAPPY

Pedicures may seem like a luxury, but happy feet make for a happy woman. (If your feet are uncomfortable or even painful, the first place where it will show up is in your expression.) Foot treatments have practical benefits, too. 'Feet that aren't cared for can develop problems like calluses, corns and ingrown toenails,' observes star Los Angeles pedicurist, Goro Uesugi. Reflexology takes that one stage further; therapists believe that healthy feet can help maintain total body well-being. So get your Health Spa at Home off on the right foot.

PLAYING FOOTSIE

Reflexology, the ancient Chinese therapy that links every organ in the body to a reflex point on the sole of the foot, is now widely recognised as an effective alternative therapy. But you don't have to be an

> There are 72,000 nerve endings that finish up in each foot, so even hitting the wrong spot will send waves of pleasure throughout a weary, stressed body!

expert to experience the benefits of rubbing the soles of your feet. There are 72,000 nerve endings that finish up in each foot, so even hitting the wrong spot will send waves of pleasure throughout a weary, stressed body! Massaging your own feet is the perfect way to relieve them if they're sore and aching. (If ignored, tired feet result in bad posture and even backache.)

• Start by rubbing oil (almond, sunflower, safflower or grapeseed oil) over your bare feet.

- Place the fatty pads ('heels') of your hands on the middle of the top of one foot and wrap your fingers underneath. Breathe in, and as you breathe out, slide the hands out towards the sides of the foot, press- 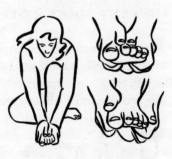 ing your fingers into the sole. Repeat five times. Then rotate the thumbs in a small circle over the top of your foot, breathing out as you lean into your thumbs. Pay attention to any painful areas and return to them after you've covered the whole foot.
- Wrap your hands around your foot as before, but this time use your thumbs to glide up the furrows between each toe, from the toe joints up to the ankle area.
- Breathe in, then out, and (resting your foot on your knee so you can access the underneath of the foot) place your thumbs on the sole. Leaning into your thumbs, rotate in small circles, covering the sole of the foot.
- Keeping your foot steady, pound the sole and sides of your foot with a gentle fist. Pay special attention to the heel. Keep the wrist flexible and your fist close to the foot.
- Keeping your foot on your knee, karate chop the sole of your foot with the side of your hand. Keep your wrist and hand relaxed, to avoid jarring.
- Wrap your forefinger around the side of each toe, in turn. Squeeze, pull away from you and gently stretch, twisting at the same time. Finish with a firm tug.
- Repeat the sequence on the other foot.

INSTANT FOOT FIX-ITS

After you've finished your basic massage, it's time to zone in on specific reflexology points. Look at the list and use the tips of your thumbs to stroke deeply – or knead – the reflexology points marked on the chart, for a minute or two each.

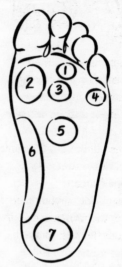

1 For tension in the back of the neck. (You can also try massaging the thinnest part of your big toe, which corresponds to the neck, too.)
2 To soothe jangled nerves.
3 To encourage positive thoughts, increased oxygen and uplifted spirits.
4 To take the weight of the world (and aches) from your shoulders.
5 To tap into hidden reserves of energy.
6 To de-tense the entire top half of your body.
7 To ease aches and pains in the lower back.

THE ULTIMATE PEDICURE

There's something infinitely glamorous about immaculately painted toenails so, now your feet are relaxed, pamper them with the perfect pedicure. Your countdown to prettily painted toes starts here…

• First, remove all traces of polish with remover.
• Use a granular scrub over your foot and up the ankle and calf, to remove dead, scaly skin; this will help your moisturiser sink in. Exfoliating pastes were used in Egypt as early as

> *Exfoliating pastes were used in Egypt as early as 1550 BC to deliver fresh blood to the skin and banish roughness*

1550 BC to deliver fresh blood to the skin and banish roughness. Today, there are many excellent ones on the market, often featuring camphor, menthol or peppermint – which are all terrific foot-soothers – but, alternatively, you can use a handful of rough sea salt.

- A key element of a good pedicure is soaking your feet to soften the skin – 10 minutes is optimum. Add a little scented bath oil (not bubbles), almond oil, wheatgerm oil or jojoba oil to the water, to moisturise the skin – especially the cuticles – and a drop of tea tree essential oil, nature's miraculous antiseptic.

- While skin is soft and moist, remove calluses by gently rubbing a synthetic pumice stone (best for hard calluses), or a natural one, around the heel in a circular motion. Pay attention to the balls of your feet, too, where skin build-up – especially during the summer, sandal-wearing months – is quickest. You can also buy a foot file, with a sandpapery surface, which quickly scuffs away hard skin. (The Body Shop do a terrific one.)

- File the nails straight across – just behind the tip of the toe. (Be careful not to cut nails too short; this can lead to soreness and infection.) Clippers, although easy to use, can split or break nails, or leave jagged corners that can encourage toenails to in-grow.

- Apply a special cuticle oil – or again, use almond or jojoba oil – to your cuticles. Leave for a moment then *gently* push them back, using a rubber-tipped 'hoof stick' (available in pharmacies), or an orange stick dipped in cotton wool.

(Whisk small fibres of cotton wool around the stick like candy floss.) Don't ever push the cuticles back so far that they reveal the little 'half-moon'.

- Massage feet and calves using a rich body cream. On the calves, use long, powerful strokes, always in the direction towards the heart. On the feet, circular movements are fine. Really knead the arches and the balls of your feet, which take a real pounding: your feet have to absorb the stress of up to twice your body weight.
- Using a cotton ball dipped in warm water, wipe away any excess oil from the nail area, then make sure your nails are completely dry.
- Using a special 'toe-divider', separate the toes. (Alternatively, weave a paper handkerchief between your toes.)
- Apply a special base coat. Then, working from big toe to little toe, apply the varnish of your choice. Paint one stripe up the middle, then one on either side. Apply two coats – allowing 4 minutes for each to dry – before completing with a special top coat. (Using products tailored for each purpose will prolong the life of your pedicure.)
- When you're finished, stick a tiny piece of cotton wool on the end of an orange stick, dip it in nail varnish remover and wipe away any excess polish.
- Just as effective as a spray-on quick-dry is to wait until nails are touch-dry (a couple of minutes), and then carefully rub a drop of jojoba or almond oil into each toenail. Not only will this harden the polish, almost miraculously, but it'll help keep those cuticles soft.

Note Do your pedicure early in the evening, otherwise it can be disturbed when you towel-dry after your bath, or get imprints from the sheets as you sleep. Using the oil to 'set' the pedicure, or a quick-dry, prevents smudging.

That great style-setter the Duke of Windsor once said: 'Only two rules really count. Never miss an opportunity to relieve yourself; never miss an opportunity to rest your feet.'

8.30 P.M. EYE BRIGHTENER

At the end of a frazzled week, your eyes need a rest – especially if they've been staring at a VDU screen. Here are some store-cupboard and fresh-from-the-fridge eye brighteners to put the sparkle back …

> *Store-cupboard and fresh-from-the-fridge eye brighteners can put the sparkle back…*

Cucumber Place a fresh slice over each closed eye and relax for 10 minutes, lying down; or squeeze the juice from half a grated cucumber and use as an eye bath.

Cold tea Steep 2 tea bags in cold water, squeeze out excess liquid and place over the eyelids; keep on for 10 minutes, lying down. Any regular tea bags will do; among the herbal range, choose only chamomile for the eyes.

Potato Grate a raw potato and put a teaspoonful or two on a square cut from a paper tissue, big enough to cover both the lid and under-eye area of each closed eye. Leave on for 15 minutes; splash with cold water. (Good for puffiness.)

Fig Also good for puffiness: halve a fresh fig and put a piece under each eye; lie down and leave for 15 minutes.

If you have any **witch hazel**, this works wonders, too; put the witch hazel in the refrigerator to chill it, then soak two cotton wool pads in the liquid. Squeeze hard (you don't want any liquid to get in the eyes), and leave on the eyes for 15 minutes.

9.00 P.M. PUT BACK THE GLOW

What you'll need...
- Oatmeal and/or cornmeal
- Honey

Facial exfoliants blitz the accumulation of dead cells that cause skin to look dull or flaky

Facial exfoliants blitz the accumulation of dead cells that cause skin to look dull or flaky; they are one of the quickest treatments for improving the appearance of your skin. The simplest exfoliants are made from finely ground grains such as oatmeal or cornmeal. (Some make-your-own cosmetics books recommend using crushed nuts – such as almonds, apricot kernels or walnuts – but these are too harsh for facial skin, which can literally be 'scratched' by the sharp corners of the nut crumbs.)

To make your own facial scrub, combine two parts of finely ground oatmeal with one part of finely ground cornmeal; if you've sensitive skin, leave out the cornmeal. (If the grains aren't ground finely enough, put them inside a sandwich bag and roll a rolling pin backwards and forwards over the bag until you've created more of a powder.) Mix two teaspoons of the oats with one teaspoon of honey, and gently massage this (somewhat sticky!) paste on to damp skin. When you've finished, rinse your skin with warm water. A gentle facial scrub like this can be used daily for oily or normal skin, and two or three times a week for dry skin.

9.15 P.M. FRAGRANCE MEDITATION

Do you have a favourite fragrance? It's good for much more than dabbing on your pulse points. You can learn to use it as an anytime, anyplace, anywhere short-cut to tranquillity. Behavioural psychologist Susan Schiffman, PhD, professor of medical psychology at Duke University Medical Centre in Durham, North Carolina, USA, has evolved a mood management technique using the favourite perfume you or I might wear every day. You simply need a back-supporting chair and a scent you love.

Do you have a favourite fragrance? It's good for much more than dabbing on your pulse points. You can learn to use it as an anytime, anyplace, anywhere short-cut to tranquillity

Sitting in the chair, take three deep, languid breaths. Envision breathing relaxation in, tension out. In turn, stretch, tense, then relax your toes, legs and tummy. Make fists, flex your biceps Schwarzenegger-style – then relax. Shrug your shoulders. Scrunch your eyes and forehead – take a deep breath, and relax. Then bring your fragrance to your nose, inhale it deeply – and try to maintain that sense of peace and quiet. Tell yourself that next time you smell the fragrance, this relaxed feeling will be recreated. (For optimum benefits, Schiffman got her subjects to repeat the exercise once or twice daily – and found that it took between just one and ten sessions before relaxation became a dead-cert trigger response when they smelled the scent in future.)

During your spa weekend, you may also want to burn scented candles – or place drops of essential oil on an aromatherapy burner, diffuser, or in a pan of water – as a mood-shifter. (see Clear the air, Saturday 2.30 p.m. on page 88, for suggested oils.)

9.30 P.M. AQUACADABRA!

Your fabulous fragrant finale to the first day of your health spa weekend is an aromatherapy bath that will waft you to sleep and set you up for the 48 hours ahead. Aromatherapy is nothing new – even though it's a buzzword in the beauty world at the moment, with the word 'aromatherapy' splashed across all kinds of products that have the merest whisper of essential oils in them. The practice of aromatherapy dates back to Ancient Egypt. There, fragrance wafted into every aspect of daily life, and was used in everything from cosmetics to embalming the mummies! The Greeks used essential oils, too – indeed, Hippocrates prescribed a daily soak in a scented bath, followed by a fragrant aromatherapy massage. (If *only* …)

At last, research has begun to back up what aromatherapists have always believed: that essential oils have a genuine effect on the body and on the psyche – their power isn't just 'all in the mind'. Robert Tisserand, one of the UK's leading aromatherapists, has been

> *Beta brainwaves –*
> *which indicate a state*
> *of heightened awareness*
> *– are increased when*
> *stimulating oils like*
> *black pepper, rosemary*
> *or basil are inhaled*

studying the effects of various essential oils on brain-wave patterns. The studies have shown that beta brainwaves – which indicate a state of heightened awareness – are increased when stimulating oils like black pepper, rosemary or basil are inhaled. And the traditionally calming oils – neroli, jasmine, lavender and rose – trigger more alpha and theta brainwaves, which are a clue to relaxation and a sense of wellbeing. What is now being recognised, too, is that essential oils enter the bloodstream – and that's why they work to relieve a variety of physical conditions, from fighting coughs and respiratory infections to relieving period pains.

ESSENTIAL OIL ESSENTIALS

There are several ways to enjoy the benefits of aromatherapy – even in daily life. Just peel an orange, and you'll release a spray of essential oils from the fruit's skin, which could combat anxiety. Or crush some mint leaves outside your back door; their aromatic oils (a.k.a. 'volatile oils') will drift towards your nose – and find their way into your brain, where they can help combat depression.

The resin, bark, roots, flowers, leaves, seeds, wood and fruit of plants all contain essential oils, although enormous quantities are often needed to deliver up just a tiny amount of oil. It takes a ton of rose petals, for instance, to make just an ounce of rose oil (which is why pure rose oil is one of the most expensive oils around). Today, essential oils are widely available in most health food stores (your friendly neighbourhood health food store is an essential pit-stop if you're going to explore the world of relaxation and wellbeing), but for mail order supplies, see Resources.

Because of their potency, though, there are some do's and don'ts when it comes to using essential oils. So the following guidelines and ideas will help you make your aromatherapy experience not only uplifting – but safe.

Remember that a little goes a long way. Some oils can trigger irritation in some individuals. Before using an essential oil, you should ideally do a patch test (see page 30), especially if you have a sensitive skin or a history of allergies.

Experiment: find the oils that are right for you. Try mixing together two to four oils to tailor-make your perfect personal blend. Aromatherapists believe that at any one time we will be drawn to the oils that our body/mind needs right then – so sniff them, and use the oils which most appeal to you at that moment. (If you really get into aromatherapy, you'll find it interesting to discover that different brands of what seems to be an identical oil may not smell alike; the smell may depend on where they were grown – soil type, and so on – and how they were harvested. As a result, they may yield subtly different effects.) You may want to steer clear of particular oils because you don't like the memories they trigger. (A fussy old aunt who smelled of lavender, for instance!) Play around with different oils to find the ones that suit you – and your memories ...

Keep all essential oils away from the eyes – and from children. And don't take them internally, unless you take the advice of a healthcare professional.

Don't use essential oils in pregnancy without taking advice first. Again, better safe than sorry: some oils are perfectly safe for use in pregnancy, but it's essential to consult a trained aromatherapist about which ones you can use.

SCRUB-A-DUB TUB-TIME

The bath is the perfect place to exfoliate skin. A scrub has one purpose: it removes dead skin cells and allows a gleaming new layer to surface. Softer exfoliators (like sponges and flannels) can be used all over; scratchier ones should be used only on rough elbow, knee and heel skin. Exfoliate before you soak: soaking softens the skin, making exfoliators over-efficient.

- Most ecological of all is a good old flannel – but these should be boiled every couple of days. (Germs like to lurk in warm flannels, whereupon the flannels not only smell like mouldy old socks but can spread infections too.)
- Natural sponges are light scrubbers (but try to make sure

that yours comes from a sustainable source – check the label when you buy). There is a new synthetic kind, from Aveda, which is barely distinguishable from the genuine article – and more ecologically sound. They dry quickly and don't mildew. (See Resources.)

- Look for agave cloths in some health food stores. These are made out of woven strands from the agave plant, a desert plant which produces string-like fibres that are wonderful for exfoliating skin.
- Loofahs are dried plants, members of the cucumber family. There are foot-long loofahs, loofahs-on-a-stick, hand loofahs – whichever you prefer.
- Pumice stones remove calluses on feet, elbows and knees. Soak the stone and skin first, before rubbing. Real pumice is porous and light enough to float in the bath; it's made of volcanic lava that has solidified and been permeated with gas bubbles.

After you've exfoliated, soak in your aromatherapy bath.

AROMATHERAPY BATH

Baths, of course, are ideal places to enjoy the mood-enhancing pleasures of aromatherapy oils. (The element of water has natural links with sensuality, too, so any time you want to indulge or boost that side of your nature, try an 'aphrodisiac' bath!) In an aromatherapy soak, some of the oil will be absorbed by the skin, while the rest evaporates into the air, and when breathed, either relaxes or revives – depending on the oil used. Simply add a few drops neat and undiluted to warm-but-not-hot water – it'll evaporate if the water's too hot – and swish. Alternatively, if you have sensitive skin, blend the essential oils into a tablespoon of avocado, grapeseed, apricot-kernel or almond oil (these are known as carrier oils) , and pour into the tub. Swish through the water with your hand ...

Some oils are uplifting, some calming. Any of these oils – together or singly – will help waft you to sleep.

Clary sage is renowned for its ability to put you in touch with 'the dream world'; a few drops in an evening bath will encourage dreams and their recall. This is a wonderful 'escapist' oil.

Jasmine, as well as being powerfully anti-depressant and an aphrodisiac, gives you confidence in your own physicality and ability to do things; it also helps open you up to beauty, music, poetry.

Juniper is for when you feel swamped by the demands of people around you; a few drops will help you break through. It's purifying and antiseptic, too. (If you don't like the smell, try blending it with grapefruit oil.)

Neroli helps open the door to your creativity and is a potent anti-depressant; like water itself, it's linked with purity and euphoria. (And a little goes a very long way ...)

Patchouli stimulates the nervous system, so it's good for a pick-you-up.

Rose is a powerful aphrodisiac, linked with facilitating creativity and sensuality in all forms; it's a highly feminine oil, and a tonic.

Ylang-ylang, a voluptuous oil with an exotic, sweet perfume, is soothing to the skin and is good to use in case of sexual difficulties. (According to aromatherapists, it also helps dispel jealousy!)

(To discover the effects of other essential oils, see Breathe Deeply and Relax, Saturday 10.00 a.m., page 65)

Soak for 20 minutes to maximise the benefits of the aromatherapy bath. Jack Mausner, PhD, Director of Research Development for Chanel, explains that while showering dehydrates the skin, bathing has the opposite effect – and 20 minutes is the optimum soak.

> *Soak for 20 minutes to maximise the benefits of the aromatherapy bath*

'Large volumes of water pounding the skin remove the natural moisturising elements – amino acids, sugars, carbohydrates and polypeptides – that are responsible for holding moisture in the skin. These very elements are enriched by taking a 20-minute hydrating bath.' And the calming effect is no placebo; blood pressure drops in the tub. One caution: 'If you spend *longer* than 20 minutes in the tub,' explains Dr Mausner, 'you'll not only end up dehydrated, but you'll also have orange-peel skin.' So, when time's up (keep a battery-operated clock on a shelf near the bath), rise slowly and cautiously from the water, to avoid losing your balance through wooziness.

Holistic therapists advise allowing skin to dry naturally; envelop yourself in towels and lie flat on the floor for up to 20 minutes. (Works wonders on the spine.) It is then time to seal in the remaining moisture with your favourite, most luxurious body moisturiser, top-to-toe. No skimping!

BEAUTIFUL BATH BLENDS

Keep a copy of this list and use it to prescribe aromatherapy baths during the week. You can target a particular emotional or physical state – and use essential oils to get you there …

For an uplifting effect, try citrus essentials, like grapefruit or lemon.
To induce sleep, experiment with chamomile, neroli or valerian.
An enliven-a-tired-body blend: add 2 drops of rosemary, 2 drops of clary sage, 1 drop of lemon.

To nourish the body – and spirit, add 2 drops of lavender, 2 drops of neroli, 1 drop of geranium and 2 drops of bergamot (which allegedly coaxes you out of depression and enlivens your sex life!)

To stimulate, add 4 drops of rosemary, 4 drops of pine and 2 of orange.

For a refreshing bath, add 2 drops of bergamot, 2 drops of lemon, 1 drop of lemon grass. (Then at the end of your bath, try turning on really cold water in the shower four or five times – for a second each time – to get circulation going and wake you up.)

For an aphrodisiac bath, add 4 drops of sandalwood, 1 drop of ylang-ylang, 1 drop of clary sage.

For a mind-sharpening bath, add 4 drops of grapefruit, 2 drops of mandarin and a drop of lemon.

For a soporific bath, add 2 drops of clary sage, 2 drops of lavender and 2 drops of marjoram.

As a tonic, after illness, add 2 drops of juniper, 3 drops of lavender and 1 drop of rosemary.

MAKE IT INTO A RITUAL

Take your portable, battery-operated CD player and favourite CDs or tapes into the bathroom with you, along with any (or all) of your candlesticks. Light the candles – and bathe by candlelight. The flickering flames, combined with the fragrance of the aromatherapy oils, help waft you to paradise.

SONGS TO STEAM BY

- I'm Gonna Wash that Man Right out of My Hair (South Pacific, 1942)
- Hot Water (Level 42)
- Splish, Splash, I was Taking a Bath (Bobby Darin, 1958)

- Singing in the Rain (Gene Kelly)
- I'm Forever Blowing Bubbles
- Handel's Water Music

BATHTIME RELAXATION EXERCISE

Any time you find your mind wandering to shopping lists and deadlines in the bath, try this technique to float cares and worries away. Using a pillow – improvised from a towel, or a specially designed rubber bath pillow – submerge your body from the neck down in the warm water. Close your eyes and let out a big, long sigh. Then gently imagine the tension releasing from your body, starting with your forehead, moving down the body to arms, fingers and toes. Breathe deeply, calmly, evenly. Then visualise any anxieties that swim into your mind as 'bubbles'. As they rise to the surface of your consciousness, let them drift up and away; imagine that you're watching the bubbles disappear over the horizon. In a few minutes, you should experience a sense of deep peace and rest. When you feel ready, get up slowly and dry yourself thoroughly. You'll be amazed how much rosier the world looks and how you feel empowered to handle the problems that seemed so overwhelming before...

10.00 P.M. MIND/BODY JOURNAL

Before bedtime, settle back in a comfy chair and let your mind roam over the treats you've already experienced; it's all part of the unwinding process. Try not just to chronicle what you did, but look at how you felt when you experienced the different activities and treats. This will help steer you towards what you might like to explore and develop in future. Take a piece of paper and a pen and, in words, reflect on your feelings about the evening. Remember that the more descriptive and detailed your writing, the more you will remember when life's back to its normal breakneck pace …

10.15 P.M. BED:
THE SLUMBER ZONE…

If there's something you're desperate to watch on TV this weekend, ask a friend to video it for you. Watching TV, in bed in particular, can over-stimulate the mind. Instead, read till you get tired. Then just before you go to sleep, try this simple relaxation treat: press the tip of your tongue against the back of your front teeth. Hold strongly for at least two minutes. You will start to feel tingling in your arms, legs – and then a wave of tingling over your entire body. Release your tongue, close your eyes – and drift off …

ZZZZZZZ…
OR, HOW TO SLEEP LIKE A BABY

Sleep, like sex and money, is something most of us would like more of. So are you getting enough? Supposedly, we spend about a third of our lives asleep. And sleep is one of our most vital tools for looking good and feeling great. (It's not called beauty sleep for nothing!) Without it, we soon start to look raddled.

> *Sleep, like sex and money, is something most of us would like more of. So are you getting enough?*

But *why* do we need sleep? (Just think what we could get done if we didn't have to shut down our systems every night). Sleep helps you relax (which might sound obvious, but so many of us have problems finding even a moment of quiet and vital calm during the waking day). Sleep gives the body and its protective immune system the chance to restore, boost and heal itself. Cell renewal generally takes place overnight. (You may think it's your skin cream that's working its magic to make your complexion look fresh as a baby's bottom in the a.m., but actually it's your own body.) When the body doesn't have to use its energy digesting and absorbing foods, thinking or exercising, it can concentrate on restoring itself, ready for the next day's demands and deadlines.

Everyone's natural body clock is different, and that's why some of us need more sleep than others. There's no point worrying that you're not getting your eight-hour quota every night if you only need six or seven! In fact, most adults sleep for about seven-and-a-half hours. Not surprisingly, the largest group who complain of sleep deprivation are women combining full-time jobs with raising young children – juggling that with housework and trying to look good!

Even people who usually sleep like a baby *sometimes* have problems sleeping. So here are some eas-zzzzz-y strategies that should ensure you get your proper quota of beauty sleep – not just during your health spa weekend, but *every* night …

GOLDEN RULES FOR A GOOD NIGHT'S SLEEP

Exercise

Try to fit in at least an hour of exercise a day, preferably out-doors – walking's fine, and that's just what you'll be doing this weekend. (See Walking Back to Happiness, Saturday 10.45 a.m., page 68.) It's often stress hormones that keep us tossing and turning (worrying about deadlines, balance sheets, unfinished projects), but exercise helps to stop the build-up of stress hor-

> *Exercise helps to stop the build-up of stress hormones in the system*

mones in the system. Before you go to bed, do some gentle stretching or yoga to melt away the built-up tension in your muscles. You'll find you sleep much more soundly.

Colour your world

If your bedroom's pillar-box red or Gothically purple, that might be banjaxing your chances of good sleep. Colours can have a dramat-

> *Soothing colours help muscles to relax, reduce anxiety and aggression, and encourage relaxation*

ic effect on our moods and wellbeing. It's no coincidence that many bedrooms are decorated in the pastel elements of the spectrum. These soothing colours help muscles to relax, reduce anxiety and aggression, and encourage relaxation. Most relaxing of all: pink. This is *not* the weekend to get out ladder, paintbrush and paint and start to redecorate, of course – but if you become aware that your bedroom may not be as restful as you'd like, you can plan to change that in the future.

Check your mineral intake

Mineral deficiency can lead to insomnia. Getting enough calcium, magnesium, zinc and potassium is particularly important. For future reference, here are good food sources for these sleep-better minerals:

Calcium: broccoli, legumes, green leafy vegetables, nuts, seeds, peas, lentils. (These sources of calcium are more 'accessible' to the body than milk products, the traditional sources)

Magnesium: nuts, shrimps, soya beans, whole grains, green leafy vegetables (magnesium is a component of chlorophyll, so the greener the vegetable, the more magnesium)

Potassium: fruit and vegetable juices and soups; salt substitutes (from health food stores)

Zinc: fresh oysters, ginger root, pecans, split peas, brazil nuts, non-fat dried milk, egg yolk, wholewheat rye, oats, peanuts, lima beans, almonds, walnuts, buckwheat, hazelnuts, green peas, shrimps, turnips, parsley, potatoes, garlic, wholewheat bread, carrots, beans, raw milk and corn

Take a good look at your bed ...

If you suffer from sleep problems, changing your bed could be the solution. (Again, make a *plan* to shop for a new bed – don't tear yourself away from your spa weekend to hit the bedroom showrooms!) Many people change their car every three or four years, their TV every five or six, their fridge and washing machine every six to eight. Beds, on the other hand, are expected to last a lifetime. But they don't. How long should a bed last? Around ten years, for a good bed, is a guideline.

Get sleep taped ...

Have trouble drifting off to the Land of Nod? Try some relaxation techniques before lights-out. There are plenty of excellent New Age-y relaxation tapes on the market, which you can play on a bedside tape player – or a Walkman, if you're worried about waking your partner.

One last pee ...

Visit the loo last thing at night. That way you're less likely to be awoken during the night by a bladder that feels like it's about to burst.

Get between the covers …

… of a good book. But don't pick a spine-chiller or a thriller for your bedtime read. A dreamy romance is more likely to get you in the mood for sleep!

Throw open your windows

Stuffy rooms are one trigger for night-time tossing and turning. Ensure the bedroom's well ventilated, and keep the heating turned down low – or preferably off. (Even if the window's open only an inch or so in winter, it can make all the difference in the world.) If you're worried about getting hypothermia, layer on the clothes and bedclothes instead. Always choose natural fibres for your night-wear and bedlinen. (There's nothing like a bolt of lightning from a nylon nightie to wake you up at 2 a.m.) You may look like Rip Van Winkle in your night-cap and socks, but you'll sleep like him, too …

> *Stuffy rooms are one trigger for night-time tossing and turning*

Dine early

Eat early. (Remember how dreamily you used to sleep when you were a kid, in the days when you sat down to your tea just after school? There's a hidden message there.) You may initially feel drowsy after a late meal, but if you go to bed on a full stomach you're likely to find it hard to drift off. The body has to work extra hard to digest a heavy evening meal, as functions tend to slow down towards the end of the day. Try to eat your last meal of the day at least two hours before you slink under the covers, and choose light, easy-to-digest foods like pasta, pulses, grilled chicken or fish with

> *Try to eat your last meal of the day at least two hours before you slink under the covers*

lightly cooked vegetables. Take your time over your supper and chew everything thoroughly, to help digestion. Avoid anything heavy or with lashings of cream – and beware: spices can keep you awake, too. That takeaway vindaloo which seemed such a brilliant idea on the way home from the wine bar will exact its revenge more effectively than the Terminator. Don't finish off your meal with a caffeine drink. (Avoid even decaffeinated coffee, which still contains a percentage of caffeine.) In fact, if you're regularly having trouble sleeping, give up caffeine after about two in the afternoon.

Snack attack

If you suffer from late-night starvation, choose a sleep-promoting food which has naturally high levels of the amino acid tryptophan (which triggers the production of calming serotonin in your brain). Tryptophan-rich foods include bananas, wholemeal crackers, tuna, lettuce, yoghurt, peanut butter and dates. What to avoid: chocolate, sugar, salty foods, cheese (which will make you thirsty), aubergine, spinach and tomatoes (which can be stimulating to the system).

Freshen the air ...

Positively charged ions in the air can be the reason you feel inexplicably tired and tense; they are also thought to contribute to migraines, headaches and breathing difficulties. This is confusing, because positive ions *sound* like they ought to be good for us, while in fact they're the 'bad guys' in the air; what we really want more of is *negatively* charged ions, which can have an invigorating, as opposed to an energy-sapping, effect. Plug in an ioniser near your bed, and this will pump out healthy negative ions into the bedroom atmosphere – helping you to breathe and sleep more easily. If you have central heating, balance a saucer of water on top of the bedroom radiator, or invest in a humidifier. (Your skin will love you for it, too. Think of how you don't have to wear so much moisturiser when the weather's sultry…)

Don't drink!

It's a complete myth that alcohol will help you sleep. True, a very small quantity of alcohol is a relaxant, but if you have more than half a glass or so, while you may drift easily off to sleep, you'll find yourself wide awake at 2 a.m. as the kidneys and liver whirr into overdrive, trying to digest a Crème de Menthe *frappé*.

Natural ways to sleep better

If you're suffering from sleeplessness, don't automatically reach for the sleeping pills. These should be a last, not a first resort, and there are plenty of other effective techniques to induce sleep.

Bach Flower Remedies

These are gentle flower and plant extracts which are taken orally – just a few drops, on the tongue – and can be used by anyone. They're available through health food stores, and they're wonderful for easing worries or irritations that might be triggering your sleeplessness.

- Try Vervain, if you've been overworking and are over-excited.
- If you're tired and exhausted but still can't sleep, try Olive.
- If you have persistent worries, or your mind's racing, White Chestnut can help.

Note These remedies can be taken in combination, if your problem's more complicated! You can usually pick up a useful free leaflet about Bach Flower Remedies wherever they're on sale. See Resources for where to find out more about them.

CHAPTER FIVE

Saturday Morning

7.30 A.M. RISE AND SHINE

Try to set your alarm for the same time you get up during the week. It might be tempting to sleep late, but this interferes with your body clock, and you can end up with 'sleep lag' by

> *If you want to grab some extra sleep, go to bed earlier than usual*

Monday morning. If you want to grab some extra sleep, go to bed earlier than usual, instead. Allow yourself half an hour in bed with an undemanding book and a cup of herbal tea or hot water.

8.00 A.M. YOGA – SALUTE TO THE SUN...

After enjoying your herbal tea, have a good stretch: make like a cat – in bed. Then perform the Salute to the Sun, which takes just a couple of minutes. The Salute to the Sun is, in yoga, the classic way to start the day – banishing weariness and getting all the body's energies flowing beautifully, in preparation for whatever the day's about to throw at you. It also boosts flexibility and gives every single muscle group a great stretch and workout. If you do it in a continuous flow, it'll really warm up your body.

1 Stand tall, with your feet together. Bring your palms together in a prayer position, facing upwards, at chest level. Be conscious of keeping your shoulders down.
2 Breathe in – through the nose* – and take a step to the right. Throw your arms back over your head and reach behind you, leaning back. (Be careful not to lose your balance!) Push your hips forward, keeping your feet parallel and your toes pointing forwards.
3 Exhale and bring your right foot in, so that your feet are togeth-

er. Keeping your legs straight, gently roll forwards and grip the back of your ankles, pulling your forehead towards your knees. (Don't strain; stretch only as far as is comfortable. It's astonishing how quickly you become limber if you do this stretch on a daily basis.)
4 Place your palms on the floor in preparation for the next move. (Don't panic if you can't manage it with straight legs – just bend your knees slightly until you can get those palms flat.)
5 Inhaling, take your right leg back behind you. Balance on your right toes and bend your left knee, keeping that foot flat on the ground. (Imagine the position a sprinter gets into, waiting for the start of a race.)

6 Repeat the whole Salute to the Sun from start to finish on the other side (i.e., taking the left leg back behind you). Eventually, with practice, you should be able to repeat the entire exercise up to 10 times on each side.

* In yoga, it's important to breathe from the diaphragm, rather then from the chest – and to breathe in and out through the nose, not the mouth. Babies breathe naturally from the diaphragm – think of their little tummies rising and falling – but adults tend to breathe from the chest, and the more stressed-out we are, the shallower our breath becomes. When you breathe *properly* you increase lung capacity and send more oxygen into the bloodstream, revitalising and purifying the internal organs.

To learn diaphragm breathing, stand straight with your feet together, shoulders down, hands resting on your hips. Then inhale deeply and push your stomach out from the diaphragm. It'll inflate like a balloon! (The exact opposite of what most women try to achieve, most of the time!) When you breathe out, your tummy will contract again. Prepare for the Salute to the Sun with half a dozen perfect breaths like this, and concentrate on getting the sequence of breathing right while you're 'saluting'. You'll find it will energise you and calm you, all at once. The right approach to yoga is to begin slowly, practice regularly, breathe deeply, and build on the small, gradual changes that you'll soon start to notice.

YOGA – THE SECRET OF BODY WISDOM

If you enjoy your Salute to the Sun, you may want to explore the world of yoga further (If you turn to Resources, you'll see some suggested further reading.) Yoga's been around for thousands of years and was probably the first 'New

> *Yoga's been around for thousands of years ... probably the first 'New Age' relaxation technique*

Age' relaxation technique. Yoga postures (a.k.a. *asanas*) exercise every bit of the body, stretching and toning all the joints and muscles, the spine and the skeleton, as well as massaging the internal organs to make them work properly. Because it helps to release mental and physical tension, yoga not only relaxes but often results in soaring energy levels. Everyone can do yoga – even if you can't touch your toes to start with, you'll soon find that you can. Here are the golden rules for making the most of your yoga practice.

• Wear baggy, loose clothing and take off jewellery, contact lenses or specs. Keep your feet bare; it's thought that socks block the energy flow and, on bare floors, could make you slip.

- Find a warm, unstuffy room.
- Choose a comfortable place; if your floor is hard, do the entire routine on an exercise mat. If you don't have a special yoga mat – often available from sports shops – use a thick towel or blanket to make the postures more comfy.
- Try to do your exercises on an empty stomach – although you can do yoga half an hour after a light snack, or two to three hours after a full meal.
- The best times for yoga practice are first thing in the morning – as in your health spa weekend – to banish any stiffness after sleeping and kick-start the mind and body. Last thing at night is good, too, so that any stresses and tensions that have accumulated through the day can ebb away before sleeping ...

Before you do any postures or *asanas*, take about five minutes to concentrate on taking slow, deep breaths. Don't allow your mind to wander. Then stand up slowly and try the following moves, which are suitable for people of all ages and every level of fitness. The first time you go through them, be careful not to push your muscles too far since they may be cold and inflexible. Once you've done the series two or three times, your muscles should be warmer and you may be able to go into a deeper pose. But don't ever push yourself.

Resting pose: Shavasana

Lie on your back, placing cushions under your knees, head and shoulders. Relax, with your arms and legs feeling loose and heavy.

Turn your palms upwards and close your eyes. For two or three minutes, count your breaths in and out. With one deep conscious breath, try to collect your mind. Stretch, relax and sit up slowly.

Stretch forward: *Paschimottanasana*

Sit upright with your legs out loose. (Your knees can be slightly bent.) With one deep, conscious breath, try to centre your body and mind. Gently lean forwards over your legs, with your arms loosely relaxed and palms open on the floor. Stay in this position for seven slow, deep and relaxing breaths. Don't strain at all. Return to the start and centre with one deep, conscious breath.

Back stretch: *Setuasana*

Sit upright with your legs out loose. With one deep, conscious breath, try to centre your body and mind. Put your hands well behind you, with your fingers pointing towards your body. Stretch your arms and extend your chest. Don't take your head too far back; try to keep it in line with your torso. Stay in this position for seven slow, deep breaths. Return to the start. Centre with one conscious breath.

Side bends: *Trikonasana*

Stand with your feet shoulder-width apart. Centre your mind and body with one deep, conscious breath. Bend your knees slightly. Stretch up your right arm, keeping the left one relaxed by your side. Lean your right arm, torso and head *very* gently over to the left. Stay here for up to seven deep, relaxing breaths. (If it's a strain, stand straight again sooner. It'll get easier before long.) Don't ever force the position. Return to the start and centre with one conscious, deep breath. Repeat on the other side.

Spinal twist (Ardha Matsyendrasana I)

Sit upright, with your hands on your knees. Centre your mind and body with one deep, conscious breath. Pick up your right ankle with your left hand and take it over your left knee, placing it on the outside of that knee. Place both hands on the right ankle. Then rotate your torso and head round to the left side and place your left hand behind your left hip, with the fingers pointing away from your body. Sit tall. Stay in place for up to seven deep, satisfying breaths. Return to the start with both hands on your right ankle, and sag your spine inwards, to relax. Sit normally and centre with the usual deep, conscious breath. Repeat the position on the other side.

Complete the session by returning to the first resting pose (Shavasana).

YOGA MOTIONS

There are many different kinds of yoga – and though it can all seem baffling, it needn't be. Hatha yoga is the most common, a total system for health and wellbeing, combining mental relaxation with postures. It helps to build strong muscles, encourages elasticity in joints and – by breathing correctly – you're feeding the tissues with fresh oxygen. Other kinds of yoga include Raja – yoga for the mind; Mantra yoga – in which you repeat a phrase over and over again while you relax, and *Kundalini* yoga, in which you release the body's own 'serpent power', a form of energy located at the base of the spine. They all come down to the same thing: making a mind–body link through breathing and poses (of which there are 84,000 – although, happily, only 84 are considered important!). You can learn yoga from books, but if you really want to explore what yoga has to offer, it may be best to find a teacher or a class first – then practice at home when you've got the hang of it.

9.00 A.M. JUICE MEAL OR WHOLEFOOD BREAKFAST

9.15 A.M. AROMATHERAPY HOT TOWEL FACIAL

You can do this daily – not just during your spa weekend, but for ever; it's a wonderful face-waker that

> *A wonderful face-waker that enlivens the senses*

enlivens the senses, too, in preparation for the day ahead.

What you'll need:
• Lavender or geranium essential oils
• A clean washcloth or small hand towel

Add two drops of the lavender or geranium oil to a basin of hot water. Soak a small hand towel or washcloth in the scented hot water, wring out the cloth, and apply it to your face for a minute or two. Dunk the washcloth again, and repeat, wallowing in the mind-clearing experience of inhaling the fragrant oils.

9.30 A.M. BODY SPLASH

Health spas offering thalassotherapy have become extremely popular as New Age mind-and-body retreats. Thalassotherapy – from the Greek word *thalassa*, meaning sea – incorporates a variety of therapeutic treatments, all peutic treatments, all

> *The minerals and trace elements found in sea water are similar to those in our own blood plasma, making it easier for us to absorb the minerals from the water*

using one vital element: sea water. It's thought that the minerals and trace elements found in sea water are similar to those in our own blood plasma, making it easier for us to absorb the minerals from the water by osmosis – literally soaking them through the skin.

You can bring the restorative power of the sea into your bathroom and rev up your system for the day ahead. You need a pound of rough sea salt and a loofah or a body brush. Add half the salt to a warm, not hot, bath. (If the bath is too hot, you'll become tired, rather than invigorated.) Soak for at least ten minutes. Then, with the loofah or brush, rub the rest of the salt into your skin. Buff softly, without pressure, in small circles, paying extra attention to dry patches such as elbows, heels, knees. (There may be no need to exfoliate areas like shins, because shaving takes off dead surface cells, too.)

Your complexion will feel – and look – like it's glowing, thanks to the salt's exfoliating action. (Sea salt is a gentler exfoliant than some commercial ones, which can have sharp edges that minutely scratch the skin like a diamond on glass.) Rinse the salt off under a warm shower – using the shower attachment to your bath, if you don't have a shower cubicle – then gradually turn the water as cold as you can stand it. The rushing water produces negative ions (charged particles in the air) – which is why we feel so invigorated after a walk beside the sea.

Pat skin dry, gently. Then add lashings of a favourite body moisturiser, and cocoon yourself in a squishy bathrobe, if you have one, while it sinks in to drench the skin.

10.00 A.M. BREATHE DEEPLY AND RELAX ...

Learning to meditate is something that's on many a busy person's 'To Do' list but, somehow, never seems to get crossed off. 'I haven't got the *time!*' is the usual excuse. Yet fans of meditation swear that its mind-clearing powers not only put you back in charge of your life, but help to sort out priorities. You may develop a whole new perspective on what seemed urgent before you began your meditation. During your health spa weekend at home, you'll have time for several meditation sessions, and will find that it really does get easier with practice. Start with just five minutes. Then build up.

To the novice, though, the very act of trying to meditate can be stressful. You seek to empty your mind (as experts counsel) and instead it instantly fills with To Do lists, becomes preoccupied with a dive-bombing bluebottle in the next room, or your limbs develop a bad case of Lotus-position-ache. As a result, potential meditators often abandon a tension-banishing technique which, practised regularly, can keep at bay a wide range of complaints including headaches, migraine, asthma, eczema, PMS, hypertension – even heart attacks. (One London study of meditation and relaxation training for men and women at risk of coronaries found that, four years on, not only did members of the meditating group have lower blood pressure readings, they showed fewer symptoms of heart disease, less angina, and the group had a lower number of deaths from heart attack.)

Research points to a significant reduction in breathing, metabolic and heart rates during meditation. Circulation improves; muscle tension disappears. The result? Zapped stress and the ability to cope better with forthcoming activities or problems. So do-it-yourself meditation begins here.

- Try not to eat or drink for half an hour beforehand – but don't meditate *before* a meal. Hunger pangs are infinitely distracting.
- Find a quiet spot where you won't be interrupted. (If you're sharing your home health spa with a friend, do the meditation alone. It can get quite giggly otherwise; meditation and giggles don't mix well.)
- Many people find it easier to meditate in dimmed lighting or with curtains/blinds pulled.
- Lie down, or sit comfortably upright with your hands resting in your lap. (Many meditation teachers prefer the seated position to avert the danger of over-relaxation, i.e., dropping off.) Get comfortable. Creaky knees or a painful back will make you fidget.
- Imagine every part of your body relaxing: start with your scalp, moving down the body, feeling tension ebb away from your jaw, neck, shoulders, stomach, arms, fingers, feet, toes.
- The aim is to stop stimulating thoughts or niggling problems from entering your mind. The easiest way is to concentrate on one neutral or calmly pleasing thought, such as the colour blue, a cloudless horizon, a mountain vista, a sunset.
- The right breathing helps: allow it to settle into a natural rhythm. Don't try to change the pattern. One meditation technique is to focus on the breathing itself: feel the air as it enters your nostrils, moving down to fill the lungs

completely, then slowly exhale. Try to breathe from the abdomen, not the chest; feel your tummy swell as you inhale. Count slowly as you breathe in and out, taking as long to expel the breath – fully – as you did to inhale.

- In Transcendental Meditation, a simple mantra – or word – is repeated over and over again. If you have trouble focusing, choose a word you like and try this. Alternatively, there's a fun way to make up your own mantra: simply open the tele-phone directory at random, close your eyes, and put your finger on the page. Take the first syllable of the surname that your finger's resting against as the start of your mantra. Turn, again at random, to another part of the book, and repeat. You will end up with a two-syllable mantra all of your own!

- Whenever a distracting thought breaks in, simply acknowl-edge it and let it go. (A helpful hint from American meditation master Ram Dass is to transform each thought into a cloud and watch it float away in your mind's eye.)

- When you've finished, slowly open your eyes, then stretch and wait a minute or two before standing up, to avoid dizziness.

- Start small. Five minutes, then ten, then as long as you want or can carve out of your schedule. (When you become practised you can meditate almost anywhere: on public transport, at your desk. If you find, during your spa weekend, that meditation is a helpful technique for you, try to establish a regular time each day for meditation so that it becomes part of the rhythm of your life. If you're a mum, try to find a few minutes before the family gets up or after they're tucked up in bed. Otherwise, interruptions are almost inevitable.)

- Some meditation masters start and finish each session by the ringing of a small hand-bell. The sound of a bell that resonates beautifully can be wonderfully calming. I was lucky enough to find, in an antique shop, a beautiful, extremely

inexpensive brass bell, giving a wonderfully pure and
pleasant sound, which I ring to open and close meditation.

- At first, meditation makes many people feel highly uncomfortable – physically and mentally. It *feels* like a terrible waste
of time, especially on days when you've got too much to do
in too little time. But everyone I know who meditates regularly swears that it enables them to get through the day's
business more efficiently, with less stress, and in *less* time.
So the time you spend meditating isn't wasted, at all.
- If you find you get truly restless sitting still, though, try
what's called a 'walking meditation', instead. As you walk,
just walk. Feel your feet. Be conscious of how first the heel,
then the middle of the foot, then the ball of the foot touch-
es the ground. Try not to be distracted by anything else,
but when you find your mind drifting – and at first it will, a
lot – bring it back to the simple movement of walking, and
shut out the distractions again. First of all, walk slowly, then
more quickly. See how long you can simply focus on the
awareness of your feet touching the ground. Nothing more.
- Remember, there is no right way or wrong way to meditate.
What works for *you* is the right way.

10.45 A.M. WALKING BACK TO HAPPINESS

A spa weekend isn't about going for Jane Fonda's burn, or over-
exerting yourself. It's about recharging and unwinding. But this
doesn't mean becoming a sloth – far from it; gentle exercise
will help to eliminate toxins – through the breath and through
the skin, while encouraging your digestive system (which isn't
being overloaded with junk) to work perfectly efficiently.

So forget boxercise, slid-erobics and circuit training. Throw out your snazzy (and probably sweaty) leotard. Because Nature's greatest fitness and looks booster is an activity most of us have been doing since we were around a year old – walking.

> *Nature's greatest fitness and looks booster is an activity most of us have been doing since we were around a year old – walking*

That's walking at fairly brisk pace, but nothing to have you huffing and puffing uncomfortably; you should still be able to carry on a conversation. Because unlike fast-paced walking, normal-paced walking actually burns *fat*, as well as calories, while building bone strength at the same time. So Hippocrates had it right, it seems, thousands of years ago, when he told us that walking is the best medicine. Most of us don't walk enough. According to Britain's Pedestrian Policy Group, if we aren't careful, we'll be lucky if we can do much more than waddle from the sofa to the fridge in a couple of generations' time. The average distance walked per person has plummeted by more than 20 per cent in the past 20 years, with disastrous consequences for our fitness. Large chunks of the population are now seriously at risk of heart disease, premature arthritis and osteoporosis through lack of exercise. And yet all we have to do is lace up our trainers – or our sensible brogues – and put one foot in front of the other.

During your spa weekend, you'll be taking several walks – during daylight, for safety's sake, and preferably with a friend. This isn't just safer – it alleviates the boredom. On an ongoing basis, if you decide to incorporate walking into your everyday life, it helps to find a 'walking buddy'. Then if one of you looks like chickening out because of bad weather/tiredness/looming deadlines, the other is likely to nudge you out of that rut and into your walking shoes. And you'll feel much better for it. (If you can't find a walking 'buddy', think about getting a large, energetic – and possibly fierce-looking – dog who'll regularly demand his 'walkies'!)

Start with a fifteen-minute walk, if you're not used to walking, and build up to half an hour by the end of the weekend. (You'll be taking four walks, in all.) If you're fitter, start with half an hour – and walk for longer if you feel like it. But if you're juice-fasting, you'll probably find that half an hour is more than enough.

Walking a mile in fifteen minutes – briskly, but not so fast as to challenge your anti-perspirant – you will burn about the same number of calories as you would jogging an equal distance in around eight and a half minutes

Walking a mile in fifteen minutes – briskly, but not so fast as to challenge your anti-perspirant – you will burn about the same number of calories as you would jogging an equal distance in around eight and a half minutes. (And without the risk of a wrenched back, ankle sprain or 'jogger's sag' – a newly observed phenomenon whereby the faces of joggers start to give into gravity sooner.) The real beauty of walking, though, is that it not only strengthens hips, thighs and bottom (plus arms and shoulders if you swing your arms while you walk), but speeds up the metabolic rate so that calories are burned even faster when you're back on the sofa afterwards. Better still, because the pace of activity is relatively slow, the body doesn't go into overdrive and start raiding its emergency carbohydrate stores for energy (as it might do when you're jogging). It simply gobbles away at unsightly fat reserves. (Like the back of your thighs …) If you consciously tighten your abdominal muscles during your walking workout, you will get extra spot-targeted benefits here, too.

But perhaps the best thing of *all* about walking is that you can do it well even if you were lousy at netball, flunked the hockey team and were odd-girl-out when it came to finding a tennis partner. You can start s-l-o-w, and build up entirely at your own pace. (It's often prescribed for people who've had heart surgery, or a coronary by-pass, who are recommended to 'walk a little further each day'.) Starting with one small step might lead to a giant leap in your fitness. What's more, you may get fewer sneezes and runny noses if you walk regularly. In a study of two groups of women in their thirties and forties, researchers compared a group of couch potatoes with another that walked for forty-five minutes, five days a week. The walkers reported half as many days with cold or flu symptoms as the non-walkers, and antibody levels rose steadily during the fifteen-week study. According to David Nieman, PhD, the professor of exercise science who headed the study, 'Walking seems to prime the body's immune system, preparing it to fight disease-causing organisms before we even feel the first sniffle.'

Use your 'spa' walks as mind-clearing exercises, helping to banish the week's woes. For 40,000 years, the aboriginal people of Australia have gone on walkabouts, wandering the continent in long, meditative stretches, roving till the mind became clear enough for them to solve their problem. As you step out – never mind a trek to Ayers Rock, a twenty-minute stroll around the block will do – your brain releases calming endorphins, easing stress and anxiety; walking can even lift mild depression. According to Dr Herbert de Vries, director of the exercise laboratory at the University of California, 'A vigorous walk can be more effective than 400 milligrams of tranquilliser.' If you like, as I just explained in the Meditation section, you can create your own 'walking meditation' by focusing on the steps you're taking, trying not to be distracted by traffic noises or other people. You don't *have* to chat to your friend, if you have one with you; it's lovely to walk companionably, silently, together.

WHAT'S THE BEST WAY TO STEP OUT?

• Wear supportive shoes. The beauty of walking lies in its total simplicity: expensive gear and flashy Spandex are superfluous. But if you're planning to go walkabout regularly, do splash out on a pair of supportive shoes. Essential walking-shoe features include a firm 'heel counter' (to prevent wobbling – ask a sports-shop shoe-sales assistant for advice), a bevelled heel – for steadiness as you come down on your heel – resiliency in the sole to cushion your foot, excellent support for your arches, and sturdy lacing, so that your feet won't 'roll'. Most of us have one foot bigger than the other, so always fit for your bigger foot (and if necessary, wear an extra sock on the other foot), rather than squeeze your toes into a shoe-size too small. (Adequate toe space is vital.) Heels shouldn't grip too tightly: leave enough space to fit a pencil between your heel and the back of the shoe. Half a size larger than usual may mean the difference between exquisite pleasure and total torture. When you're trying on shoes, always wear the socks you'll be striding out in. For long walks, two pairs of socks – or changing into a fresh pair mid-way – can prevent agonising blisters caused by damp-sock-rub.

• As with any form of exercise, start gently and end gradually. Just set out at a leisurely stroll and within five or ten minutes build up to a comfortable, brisk pace.

• A walking regime isn't *quite* as simple as just opening the door and striding out into the wide blue yonder. You should always start with a warm-up, and finish with a cool-down, including stretches. Stretches to prevent cramps and muscle strains before and after your walk-out include:

Heel raises – rise up on your toes, twenty times in succession

Back of thigh stretches – hold on to a stationary object with both hands, extend your left leg behind you, bend your right knee, lean forward and hold for 10 to 15 seconds; then do the same with the other leg

Calf stretch – hold on to a stationary object with both hands, extend your right leg behind, bend your left knee and lean forward; then switch legs

Knee bends – hold on to an immobile object with your left hand, bend your right knee, reach back and pull your foot towards your bottom with your right hand; then reverse

Side stretches – hold your right elbow with your left hand over your head, and with feet apart and knees very slightly bent, pull your elbow to the left; then reverse.

All these stretches should be held for 10 to 15 seconds, and repeated at least twice. Other warm-up exercises include stamping on the spot and waving your arms in opposite directions. (For more stretches, see Five Simple Stretches, Sunday 6.00 p.m., page 124.)

- Your full speed should be fast enough to make you breathe hard, but not so fast that you can't gossip away to your best friend or partner at the same time.
- Walk tall – keep your head high, your back straight and pull your stomach in. Swinging your arms in the opposite direction to your leg movements can increase calorie burn by 5 to 10 per cent.
- Make an early start – in the morning glycogen stores are low and energy's more likely to be taken from body fat.

- Gradually increase your distance. Try to aim for three miles at least three times a week.
- When the weekend's over, make a point of planning your life around your walks – walk to work if you can, or at least to the bus stop or station. If you have to take public transport, try getting off one stop/station early and walking the rest of the way. If you must drive, park a way away from your destination and walk the last few hundred yards.

Make an early start – in the morning glycogen stores are low and energy's more likely to be taken from body fat

- If you haven't walked much in years, it's a bit too ambitious to go up hill and down dale this weekend – but if you continue to walk, as part of your regular exercise regime, you'll swiftly build up to the stage where you can take to the hills without getting out of breath. If you're a practised walker, incorporate some hills into your weekend 'spa walks'. Leaning forward slightly as you walk uphill stops you straining your leg muscles and is terrific for the buttocks. When you're walking downhill, slow down a bit and take shorter steps to save your knees from injury. You'll use up more calories by walking up and down hills: someone who weighs just over 10 stone will burn 300 calories an hour walking at 3.5 miles per hour on flat ground; on a gentle hill that rises to 400 calories, and on a steep hill, to 500. Other surfaces that improve

You'll use up more calories by walking up and down hills: someone who weighs just over 10 stone will burn 300 calories an hour walking at 3.5 miles per hour on flat ground; on a gentle hill that rises to 400 calories, and on a steep hill, to 500

the calorie-burning power of your workout include sand, gravel and grass. (They're more challenging than tarmac or pavement.)
- A walk in the early evening before supper takes the edge off your appetite, and gives your energy level a little boost before the evening.
- Don't be deterred by rain/hail/sleet/icy winds. In Denmark, they have a saying: 'There's no such thing as bad weather – there's only the wrong clothes.'

Walking advertisements – literally – for the stepping out include Michelle Pfeiffer ('It burns fat and gives me energy for the day'), First Lady Hillary Rodham Clinton, actress Suzanne Somers (who calls it 'a mind-cleanser') and former tennis star Chris Evert, who has traded her tennis racket for a pair of walking shoes.

TEN-MINUTE FOOT MASSAGE

When you're back from your walk, this is the treat you deserve (and your feet will be crying out for!).

What you'll need:
- A rolling pin (or, if you have one, a special foot roller from The Body Shop)

Set aside ten minutes. Shut the door and find a comfortable chair which enables your feet to touch the ground. Take off your shoes and socks. Begin this exercise by rolling your bare or stockinged feet over the foot roller or rolling pin for at least five minutes. Keep your eyes closed and take long, deep breaths.

Now, put your right ankle on your left knee. Using your thumb and forefinger, press the tip of each toe, using a gentle pressure. Hold for several seconds and release. This is a form of acupressure which will, according to reflexologists, release tension in corresponding parts of the body. Next, press gently around the entire edge of the sole and then the heel of the foot – in spots about two inches apart. Press, hold, release.

Rub the arch of the foot in a circular motion, until you feel a warming sensation in the foot. Before long, not only will you feel relaxed, but your whole body will become toasty-warm. Repeat all of the movements on the other foot. As a finale, close your eyes and press your fingertips together for two to three minutes. (Incidentally, this is a quick pick-me-up at any time – although it may get you some strange glances if you try it in the office…)

11.45 A.M. HAIR TREATS

> *What you eat matters a lot – but so does what you clean and condition your hair with*

Most of us only have time, day to day, to wash 'n' go. But if you lavish TLC on your hair during your at-home spa weekend, you can help banish the frizzies and put back head-turning gloss.

Healthy hair looks shiny and gleaming, with a bounce to it. In fact, good condition depends more on care and attention than all the styling products in the world. What you eat matters a lot – but so does what you clean and condition your hair with. Some shampoos are so lathery and harsh they're probably more appropriate for washing your car! What's fun (and gentle on your tresses) is to experiment with making your own, with soapwort – Nature's own soap herb, which you can buy from herbalists and some health food stores. (See Resources for mail order suppliers.)

Of course, you *can* use your regular store-bought haircare for this treatment – but it's an adventure to make your own. What's more, home-made shampoos don't contain detergents that can strip away the scalp's naturally protective oils. You may think that oil is your hair's worst enemy and try to banish it at all costs – but *over*-cleansing will simply encourage the scalp to step up oil secretion, and make hair look even more greasy and limp. Better, then, to take a gentle approach, with these back-to-nature hair cleansers…

ULTRA-GENTLE SHAMPOO

- 15 g/^{1}/$_2$ oz crushed soapwort root
- 1.2 litres (2 pints) boiling water

Crush the soapwort with a pestle and mortar or grind it in a herb grinder. Make a tea of the soapwort, steeping it in the hot water for a quarter of an hour, then strain. The average head of hair will need around half a cup of the shampoo to come clean. You can make your own herbal shampoo with chamomile flowers (for fair hair) or rosemary (which is great for dandruff): add them to the tea mixture, then strain well before using.

Keep the shampoo in a plastic, screwtop bottle (an old mineral-water bottle for example) in the fridge. It'll keep for a couple of weeks that way, and there's more here than you'll use in your spa weekend.

If you can't get your hands on any soapwort, try these store-cupboard standbys …

DRY HAIR SHAMPOO

Hair and eggs go beautifully together. (But don't use too-hot water to wash off, or you'll end up with scrambled eggs all over your scalp!) For the simplest shampoo of all, take 2 egg yolks and 1 cup of water. Beat the yolks into the water, then massage into the hair and scalp for 5, scalp-stimulating minutes. Leave on for 10 minutes. That's all the shampoo you need! Alternatively, for a richer (and more expensive!) shampoo, use half a cup of water and half a cup of brandy.

OILY HAIR SHAMPOO

• 4 whole eggs
• 225 ml/8fl oz rosewater
• 225 ml/8fl oz rum

This is a two-step cleanser that's wonderful for greasy scalps.
First beat the eggs, then massage through the hair and leave
for 15 minutes; rinse off with warm water. Then add the rosewater to the rum and use this as the final rinse.

TO BEAT DANDRUFF

• 2 egg yolks
• 110 ml/4 fl oz warm water
• 2 teaspoons apple cider vinegar
• 225 ml/8fl oz tepid water

Beat the egg yolks into the warm water, and massage into the
scalp and hair. Leave on for 10 minutes, then rinse with warm
water. As a final, scalp-healing rinse, add the apple cider
vinegar to the water and pour it over your hair.

THE MAGIC TOUCH

Before you slather on your hair mask – the next step in your hair
pampering – give yourself a scalp massage. (If you've invited a
friend or loved one to share the spa retreat with you, you can
trade scalp massages. This is usually carried out most easily if
the masseur stands behind the massagee.) Start by pressing the
index and middle fingertips between the brows for a count of
five. Then repeat, every quarter inch, in a line out towards the

temples. Make small circles over the temples, for a count of 20. Then, using stiff fingers, press into the scalp and wiggle them up and down and then around in circles, moving all over the scalp, for a count of ten. Lastly, tug small sections of the hair (about half an inch up from the roots, so it doesn't hurt), repeatedly and firmly, then press the pads of the fingers into the scalp. Repeat all over the scalp. You'll feel wonderfully invigorated and uplifted. (Scalp massage is terrific, on an ongoing basis, if you use your brain a lot at work, or if you suffer from headaches.)

Scalp massage is terrific, on an ongoing basis, if you use your brain a lot at work, or if you suffer from headaches

TLC FOR HAIR

Because hair is porous, it can be easily damaged – or greatly improved – by the way you treat it. Heat-styling, chemical agents (such as perms and tints), harsh synthetic shampoos and environmental stresses such as chlorine, pollution and too much sun, can cause your hair to become dry, dull and prone to breaking. But luckily, because hair is porous, it's possible to undo the damage fast, with moisturising and strengthening elements.

Once you've massaged in your hair mask, wrap hair in a warm towel – or cover with a sandwich baggie (do check that nobody's going to barge in on you in this unglamorous state!). The heat will encourage penetration of the hair shaft, delivering the emollient ingredients where they're most needed. Choose whichever deep conditioning treatment most appeals to you …

CARIBBEAN CONDITIONER

- 3 tablespoons white rum
- 1/2 teaspoon vanilla extract
- 1 egg

Mix the rum and egg together and stir well, then add the vanilla extract. After shampooing, pour the mixture on to your hair and leave it on for a minute or two. Rinse well with the coolest water you can stand. This intoxicatingly scented treatment boosts shine, body and softness and is suitable for normal-to-oily hair; the egg softens and the rum removes oil. The vanilla not only makes the conditioner smell delectably tropical, but acts as a softener.

CANTALOUPE CONDITIONER

- 1/2 cantaloupe melon, peeled and mashed

Massage the mashed cantaloupe into your hair after you've shampooed. Leave for 10 to 15 minutes, then rinse well with warm to cool water. This is a deliciously light conditioner that's perfect if you have oily hair as it's grease- and oil-free.

ULTRA-REMOISTURISING HAIR PACK

This is done before you shampoo, rather than afterwards. You'll need:

- Jojoba oil
- A shower cap
- Rosemary and sage essential oils

This treatment will combat a lot of the damage caused by over-cleansing, heat and chemical treatments. Ideally, you should repeat it at weekly intervals, for maximum benefit. In a small container, combine a teaspoon of jojoba oil with four drops of rosemary and four drops of sage essential oils. (These are terrific scalp stimulants, too.) Massage this mixture into your scalp with your fingertips. If your scalp tends to oiliness, apply the mix only to the ends of your hair. When it's been slathered on, slip on the shower cap and let the oils stay in your hair for half an hour. Follow this treatment with your regular shampoo, lathering twice to remove the excess oil. Condition. (Then – unless you really can't dry your hair successfully without a blow-dryer – towel- and tousle-dry your hair; in daily life, we're barely conscious of the noise that hairdryers make, but during your spa weekend, you'll be seeking to reduce exposure to machine noise to a minimum, freeing you to enjoy and experience other sounds, for a change. Like the birds singing, the wind, even the rain – all of which are drowned out by whirring and buzzing of electrical goods.)

DRY HAIR TREATMENT
· ·

Again, as for the Ultra-Remoisturising Hair Pack, follow this treatment with your regular shampoo, lathering twice to remove the excess oil, and condition.

- 2 egg yolks
- 1 drop vinegar
- 1 teaspoon almond oil
- 1 teaspoon mayonnaise

Mix together in a bowl, apply to hair, and leave on for 10 to 15 minutes. (See instructions above.)

MORE STORE-CUPBOARD HAIR BOOSTERS

Use this list to remind yourself that in future, you don't always need to splash out on expensive salon treatments or hair-boosting products. You may already have the secrets of shiny hair in your larder…

Castor oil Breakable hair and split ends respond glossily to a massage with half a cup of castor oil. Then wrap a radiator-warmed towel round the head for half an hour before shampooing twice to remove the last traces of oil. (This is a far more pleasant use for this oil than being forced to guzzle it, as we often were as children!)

You don't always need to splash out on expensive salon treatments or hair-boosting products. You may already have the secrets of shiny hair in your larder...

Avocado Mash an entire avocado and use it as a hair pack. For more intensive treatment, carefully cover the hair with a supermarket shopping bag and hope that nobody rings the doorbell. Shampoo and condition as usual.

Olive oil Dry hair loves olive oil. Gently warm 2 tablespoons of olive oil (lukewarm – nowhere near hot enough to fry!) and gently massage into every last corner of the scalp. Comb through with a wide-toothed comb. Then wrap the head in a radiator-heated towel. (If you do this when you're in the bath, it'll be even more effective.) Shampoo and condition as usual.

Nettle rinse This gives the hair body. Pick a handful of roadside nettles (wear rubber gloves!) and simmer them in half a litre/a pint of water until they're soft. Strain, then dilute with an equal quantity of water. Pour over your head as the final rinse.

CHAPTER SIX

Saturday Afternoon

12.45 P.M. JUICE MEAL OR WHOLEFOOD LUNCH

1.15 P.M. TAKE A BREAK...

Give yourself 20 minutes, at least once each day this weekend, to do nothing – guilt-free. Daydream, potter, dance, paint, stare out of the window. Remember: you're setting your own schedule. If you don't feel like an activity that's on the home-spa list, skip it. (However, don't chop and change activities, as they've been carefully timed to pep you up or calm you down, to wake you up – or get you ready for sleep.)

1.35 P.M. FABULOUS FACIAL

The perfect spa weekend delivers a series of treats, challenges and rewards. Now's the time to indulge yourself with an ultra deep-cleansing facial …

Really, there is no need to splash out on expensive face masks. Most of us have the ingre-

> No need to splash out on expensive face masks. Most of us have the ingredients we need to mix our own in the fridge

dients we need to mix our own in the fridge. A growing beauty trend is to make your own cosmetics at home. Because they're made fresh – and used fast – food-based beauty goodies are ultra-natural and free from chemical preservatives, so they can be a boon to sensitive skins. (Although if your skin's touchy, you should still always try a 'patch test' first – see page 30 – to be on the safe side.) Once you get the hang of D-I-Y cosmetics, you can experiment with endless fresh fruit and vegetables and store-cupboard basics to create treats that rival, for effectiveness, many of the high-tech beauty products you'll find on the shop shelf. They're fast, they're fun – and they don't cost a fortune.

Eggs are particularly useful ingredients for at-home beauty-boosters – whatever your skin type. They work as a skin conditioner and toner, helping to reduce the appearance of pores

> *Egg whites are good for oily skins, while dry skins love egg yolks*

on the skin. The simple rule to remember is that egg whites are good for oily skins, while dry skins love egg yolks. (Used on the hair, meanwhile, eggs are oomph-giving, adding volume and thickness – see above.) The other reason eggs crop up so often in back-to-nature beauty treats is that they work as a 'binder', ensuring a smooth texture and making lotions and potions a pleasure to use.

But first things first. As beautician Lydia Sarfati, who runs Manhattan's famous Repêchage salon, observes: 'Using a mask on a dirty face is like putting polish on a dirty floor.' So as you massage in your regular cleanser, deploy lymphatic draining techniques, which help improve circulation and boost the complexion's ability to disperse toxins. With your middle fingers, press hard at these points: two inches higher than where your eyebrows begin above the nose, then just above the brows. Move fingers out two inches, then repeat the sequence. Move down the face, press on the cheekbones (near the nose), then cheeks, then chin. Move out again, deploying the same movements.

Once the skin's been prepared and cleansed, fill a basin or bowl with warm water and add three drops of lavender essential oil, which is lightly antiseptic and extremely relaxing. Make a tent over your head with a towel, and breathe the fragrant air for five minutes, as the steam opens the pores to release hidden dirt and debris – and clears your mind, at the same time.

Once you've cleansed and steamed your skin, then it's time to apply the home-made mask matched to your skin type. (Of course, if you prefer, you can use a favourite mask from a beauty company.) After you've removed your mask, sweep skin with an easy-to-make, suits-all-skin-types rosemary rinse (see below).

ROSEMARY FRESHENER

•••

- 600 ml/1 pint water   • 1 teaspoon dried rosemary leaves

Boil the water and add the rosemary for one minute, then turn the heat off and let it sit, covered, for 10 minutes. Then place it in the fridge or (if you've room) in the freezer section, while you mix your mask. Choose from these:

EGG WHITES FOR PROBLEM SKIN

•••

- 1 egg white   • 1 tablespoon mashed cucumber

Egg whites have a mildly astringent action and can work wonders on mild break-outs, while cucumber is an excellent skin-soother. Great in emergencies – or once a week, as pimple prevention!

Gently mix the egg white (don't whisk) with the cucumber, and apply as a 20-minute facial.

EGG PORRIDGE MASK FOR SENSITIVE SKIN

•••

- 10 tablespoons of oatmeal   • 110 ml/4fl oz hot water
- 1 egg white   • 1/2 apple (cored, not peeled)
- 2 heaped tablespoons plain yoghurt   • 2 tablespoons honey

In this mix, egg is mixed with skin-calming ingredients like yoghurt and honey. In addition, it uses oatmeal – which is richer in fat than other grains, restoring moisture and suppleness to even the most sensitive skins.

Combine the oatmeal and hot water and stir until you've got a smooth porridge. Allow it to stand for 5 minutes, until the water's completely absorbed and it looks like a paste. Put the remaining ingredients in a blender or food processor and whizz for 30 to 45 seconds, adding the oat mixture before blending for another 10 to 20 seconds. If you'd like a thicker texture, make more oat paste and add that. Apply it evenly to the entire face and relax for a quarter of an hour, or until the skin starts to feel tight. Rinse thoroughly with warm water and apply your usual moisturiser.

HONEY, AVOCADO AND EGG MASK FOR NORMAL-TO-DRY SKIN

• Half an avocado (peeled, with the stone taken out)
• 1 egg
• 1 teaspoon mayonnaise
• 1 teaspoon honey
• 1 teaspoon bicarbonate of soda
• 2 drops lemon essential oil (for its scent)

Eggs and avocado blend together beautifully in D-I-Y cosmetics as they're both highly moisturising. (Avocados are 20 per cent fat.) What's more, this recipe uses mayonnaise – which works to tone and smooth skin. (In a parched skin emergency, you can spoon mayonnaise straight on to your face from the jar!)

Purée the avocado, egg and mayonnaise in a blender, then add the honey, bicarbonate of soda and lemon essential oil. (Alternatively, beat it by hand, adding the bicarbonate of soda last.) This needs to be used up at once – apply any extra to the chest and neck area.

D-I-Y RADIANCE RESTORER

....

- 1 egg
- 1 tablespoon ordinary cooking oil, such as sunflower
- 1 drop lavender essential oil

Blend the egg with the cooking oil and add the lavender oil. (Incidentally, lavender is one of the only essential oils which can be used undiluted on skin, and is deserving of a place in every home's first-aid kit as a near-miraculous burn treatment.) Smooth the mixture over the face with your fingers, or a cotton ball, and languish for 15 minutes before rinsing with warm water.

Rinse off your chosen mask with the rosemary and water mix, fresh from the freezer or refrigerator. It will feel cool and tingly. (Return the freshener to the fridge, where it will keep for a few days as a home-made addition to your usual skin-care routine – or an alternative, if you already use toner, astringent or freshener). After you've removed your face mask, pat skin gently dry and apply your usual moisturiser or – if you're going outside – sun protection. (To ward off premature ageing, dermatologists recommend a minimum of Sun Protection Factor 15 – year round. Yes, even when it's cloudy. Yes, even when it's winter.)

2.30 P.M. CLEAR THE AIR

'Air is the element of spring, and of sunrise – it's linked with awakening, purity, newness, growth, excitement, inspiration, intellect and light,' says leading aromatherapist Robert Tisserand, one of the key figures in the aromatherapy world. 'If you want a fresh start, if you're seeking inspiration, problem-solving – or you simply want to feel "in love" with life again – then releasing certain oils (and blends of oils) into the air can help.' (And falling in love with life again is surely what your home-health-spa weekend is all about.)

There are many do's and don'ts in aromatherapy. (As you've discovered during your preparation for Aquacadabra, Friday 9.30 p.m., page 40.) Some oils, for instance, should be avoided by pregnant women. Others can have extremely potent effects as they're absorbed by the skin and enter the bloodstream.

However, one way for absolutely *everyone* to enjoy the oils safely is by diffusing them into the air, creating a wonderfully fragrant environment. 'Breathing essential oils is a wonderful way to experience their magic,' observes Robert Tisserand.

You can use aromatherapy oils to manage your moods, literally to shift your mindset. Use a few drops of an individual

> *Use aromatherapy oils to manage your moods, literally to shift your mindset*

oil – or tailor-make a combination, as suggested. You can use an aromatherapy burner, a diffuser – which whizzes fresh air through a filter on to which drops of oil have been placed – or simply add a few drops to a pan of boiling water, on the stove; before long, you will have fragranced the whole house. (But do remember to switch the heat off again. Burning saucepans aren't compatible with relaxation.) Alternatively, add four to six drops of essential oil to water in a plant mister; shake well and use the spray as you would any air freshener.

UPLIFTING OILS

Bergamot A good airborne antiseptic and immunostimulant (i.e., it'll help your body fight infections), this blends well with any other oil

Cardamom Mentally stimulating; also an immunostimulant. Blends well with citrus oils

Eucalyptus Cleansing, purifying, antiseptic. Blends well with kanuka, rosemary, peppermint, tea tree

Geranium Has the 'soft' air qualities; it's emotionally cleansing and blends well with rose and citrus oils

Grapefruit Refreshing, mentally uplifting. Blends well with any other oil

Kanuka Refreshing, a very good airborne antiseptic. Blends well with rosemary, peppermint, eucalyptus, tea tree

Lemon Refreshing, emotionally uplifting, good air antiseptic and an immune-booster. Blends well with any other oil

May chang Zingy, zesty, invigorating. Blends very well with citrus oils

Peppermint Excellent general stimulant, very refreshing. Blends well with kanuka, rosemary, eucalyptus, tea tree

Rosemary Excellent general stimulant and antiseptic; refreshing. Good with kanuka, peppermint, eucalyptus, tea tree

Tea tree Cleansing, purifying, antiseptic. Blends well with kanuka, rosemary, peppermint, eucalyptus

Note In addition to their therapeutic benefits, essential oils can be an effective alternative to chemical disinfectants. Try wiping kitchen counters with diluted lemon and geranium oils, or sprinkle a few drops of lemon, pine or geranium oil into the water in which you rinse your dishes.

SHOPPING FOR OILS

- If you possibly can, smell the oil before you buy it – if you don't like the smell, don't splash out.
- Buy a good quality essential oil. Essential oil is expensive; if it's cheap it's either diluted, or a poor quality oil.

- Don't buy oils which have been kept in a window or under direct lighting – these tamper with the effectiveness of the oils.
- The bottle should always be dark glass, with a screwtop (preferably child-proof) and a plastic insert in the neck which lets you pour out the oil drop by drop.

3.00 P.M. AFTERNOON WALK

Try to walk further – and maybe more briskly – than you did this morning …

4.00 P.M. AT-HOME WAXING

With all the brilliant warm or hot wax treatments on the market at the moment – many of which can simply be heated in a microwave – there's real-

> *A spa weekend is the perfect time to perfect your waxing technique*

ly no need for salon de-fuzzing. A spa weekend is the perfect time to perfect your waxing technique – which should save you time and money, in future, if you've always relied on a beautician.

- Choose a waxing kit that features beeswax. The wax is thinner and easier to use than other waxes.
- Wash your legs first, towel dry and skip moisturiser – which can interfere with the wax.
- Sprinkle talc-free powder on to legs. This will absorb oils in the skin and make the wax pull off cleanly. The powder will also show you where you've waxed – whether you have fair hair or not.

- Heat wax according to directions. (Some are microwave-able; some are heated on top of the stove.) The wax should be warm – never hot – and have the consistency of honey. Scoop wax from the top, where it's coolest.
- Start with the front of the leg. Using a wooden utensil – preferably a wooden spatula – apply wax in the same direction the hair grows, in a thin, slightly see-through strip about two inches wide and half the length of your calf.
- Press the muslin strip – usually supplied with the wax – into the wax, gently smoothing it downwards.
- When the wax has the consistency of soft caramel – *before* it hardens completely – quickly pull off the strip in the opposite direction. (To get an idea of whether the wax is ready to pull, test-pull a small corner.)
- It helps to take deep, rhythmic breaths to minimise any pain. If you hold your breath – which is a natural urge – it's worse!
- Immediately after you've pulled off the wax, apply gentle pressure to the waxed skin with the palm of your hand.
- Keep ice nearby, to alleviate any redness and swelling. (Rub it over any sore areas, as a kind of instant anaesthetic.)
- If you're making a mess, or having second thoughts, apply a body moisturiser and the wax should simply rub off.
- After waxing, spray the skin with cool water. (Use a plant mister, or one of the cosmetic water sprays made by Evian or Vichy Thermal Spa.) You can buy special post-depilation sprays and creams to smooth into the area, or add a couple of drops of antiseptic tea tree oil to your regular body lotion. (It might smell a little funny – tea tree has an odd, musty smell – but this amazing essential oil is one of the most efficient antiseptics known to medicine; in fact, it's increasingly being used in hospitals to prevent the spread of infection.)

WAXING DON'TS

Don't go over an area more than once in 24 hours, or you can trigger bleeding, swelling and bruises.

Don't boil the wax – and always test its temperature on your hand before applying to your body.

Don't have any heat treatments for 24 hours (such as saunas or steam baths) after waxing, and don't expose newly waxed skin to the sun, fragrance, deodorants or body products featuring AHAs (alpha-hydroxy acids, a.k.a. fruit acids). As you've stripped away the top layers of dead skin, along with your hair, the skin in the waxed zone is temporarily ultra-vulnerable.

Don't attempt to wax too-short hair. The longer the hair, the better the results you'll get. Ideally, your hair should be more than a centimetre – at least half an inch – long, and longer if it's very thick or coarse.

5.00 P.M. TAKE A BREAK (OR A NAP ...)

Saturday Evening

7.00 P.M. JUICE MEAL OR WHOLEFOOD SUPPER

7.30 P.M. EVENING MEDITATION

You should discover that, even just since this morning's session, you find meditation more comfortable – and you're able to clear your mind for longer.

8.00 P.M. NIGHT-TIME MILK BATH

By now, you might feel like you're squeaky clean – but there is a good reason for bathing last thing at night: a warm brain is a sleepier brain. (Remember: baths are not just for washing, but for *wafting*.) Baths are sheer liquid refreshment. Physically, the relaxing effects of a hot bath are easy to understand: warm water displaces weight, making you feel light, and as your capillaries (blood vessels) expand from its warmth, your blood pressure drops. (This is why people with heart problems are advised not to take extra-hot baths; the drop in blood pressure can put extra strain on the heart, which must then work harder to pump blood through the body.)

> There is a good reason for bathing last thing at night: a warm brain is a sleepier brain

A safe temperature for almost anyone is 90 to 95°F (32 to 35°C). You can use a cooking thermometer to determine the temperature. You'll probably want a different temperature in summer to winter. (Actually, you'll find that for re-energising, a tepid bath is best. Hot baths, although they feel good and are great for relaxing sore muscles, sedate the system rather than revive it.) One trick I learned for keeping bath temperature constant is to put a matchstick under the plug, so that the water just seeps out of the bath, while keeping the hot tap just trickling in. This isn't at all ecological, but it's probably OK for the occasional, luxurious splurge …

In the quest for tranquillity, then, we should *all* become mermaids. That *doesn't* necessarily mean splashing out on lots of expensive bath lotions and potions, either. If milk baths were good for Cleopatra,

> *If milk baths were good for Cleopatra, they're good enough for the rest of us*

they're good enough for the rest of us. (Cow's milk is a fine substitute for the asses' milk she preferred, by the way.) The Egyptian queen was definitely on to something; the fatty elements settle on the skin's surface. A store-cupboard beauty standby is to pour a litre of milk (homogenised or otherwise) in your own bath, and experience the softening effects, further enhanced by a handful of honey (which is antiseptic). Even dried milk powder will make the water more moisturising. You will feel the difference immediately. Bathing in it is like swimming in a soft, warm, white cloud. The bath doesn't smell funny, or leave you feeling sticky, as you might think it would. You'll be amazed at how milk softens the water and how satiny smooth your skin is after this protein treatment. Another skin-soothing option is putting almond oil in the bath, especially if you have to cope with hard water. Indeed, milk and almonds together make a delicious combination for the special pampering of skin and soul …

Meanwhile: to soap, or not to soap? Many skin-care professionals believe that we don't really need it and that except for hands and feet, which get really dirty, warm water will do the trick. If you do like to use soap, use one that contains humectant ingredients – Neutrogena, for instance – which won't tamper with the skin's pH, leaving it taut or parched. And whatever kind you use, rinse, rinse, rinse, otherwise residues from surfactants (the agents in soap that stop dirt and grime clinging to skin) continue to break down the skin's protective mantle, causing dryness and even inflammation.

One last tip: whenever you bathe, keep a glass of (room temperature) spring water within sipping distance, letting nature's perfect drink keep the moisture level topped up from the inside.

MORE BATH BLISS ...

There are plenty of other things you can add to your bath that will soothe skin, muscles and tired brain cells. And the good news is that you've probably got most of them in your kitchen ...

- When your skin feels flaky (and so do you), add a cup of apple cider vinegar. It's great for sore muscles or itchy skin. This is also great – in a lukewarm-to-warm bath – to soothe sunburned skin. The vinegar restores the skin's natural acid balance, which is why it helps banish itchiness.

> *When the wind's whipping in straight from the North Pole, try adding between a teaspoon and a tablespoon of powdered ginger to your bath*

- On a night when the wind's whipping in straight from the North Pole, try adding between a teaspoon and a tablespoon of powdered ginger to your bath. It will warm you up and also soothe aching, sore muscles. (So it's great post-workouts, too.) It's best to start with the smaller amount of ginger, until your body gets accustomed to the toasty effects it creates. But if you want to sweat out a cold or flu, add more.

- Lemons make the perfect, zing-y summer bath, refreshing you in hot weather. Add up to a cupful of freshly squeezed lemon juice to your bath, then throw in the skins, for good measure. It'll cool the skin, tighten pores and reduce oiliness. (But if you've got any cuts – say from rose-pruning – put a touch of Vaseline on them first, otherwise they'll sting.)

- Oatmeal is fantastic for soothing irritated skins – it's great for people who've got eczema, and it can help reduce excess oil on the skin. However, if you just chuck it in the bath it's extremely messy, so make a bath bag first: cut a piece of cotton or muslin into a handkerchief-sized square. (Or just cheat and use a hankie.) Into the centre, put in two generous handfuls of oatmeal, then gather the corners and fix them with a piece of long string, which you can use to dangle the bag from the tap so it catches the stream of water. When the bath's full, squeeze the bag from time to time to release the oats' benefits into the water.

- At times when the whole world has been gunning for you since dawn, make a bag filled with herbs, instead of oats – dried rosemary, mint, lavender or chamomile. Water running through the bag will turn your bathroom into paradise.

9.00 P.M. BE YOUR OWN MASSEUR ...

Massage is one of the greatest ways to unwind. For most of us, receiving a massage is a wonderful experience, but there will always be times when there's no one available to give you a treatment. (And besides, some people can't relax with a masseur they don't know, so the entire experience is stressful, not de-stressing.) You can, however, just as easily massage yourself. It may not be as deeply enjoyable as having someone else work on you, as you can't turn off completely, but within a few minutes you can soothe away tension, stimulate circulation – and, like all massage, help yourself relax.

Self-massage isn't a new idea. In the Orient, self-massage techniques have been handed down in families for centuries. It's also sometimes taught in schools there, as part of a stress-busting, health-promoting approach to life. The advantage, of course, is that you can focus on exactly where your own specific aches and pains are – because you're feeling them! And because you're completely in control, you can massage yourself more deeply – or go easy, depending on how you feel.

- Choose somewhere comfortable to sit – a favourite chair, or on the floor.
- Wear loose, easy clothing.
- Make sure the rest of your body – the part you won't be massaging – is in a comfortable position before you start.
- Never practise self-massage when you're tired or hungry.
- During your spa weekend, of course, you're avoiding stimulants like tea, coffee and alcohol. But if you decide to go in for self-massage more regularly, don't smoke, drink or have an energy-jolting drink for at least a couple of hours beforehand. It'll simply be too tough to unwind.

HEAVENLY HAND MASSAGE

Most of us store a huge amount of tension in our hands, just from everyday activities like typing, writing, driving. (I sometimes look down at my hands, when I *think* I'm fairly relaxed, and find that I've clenched my fists into a tight ball!) Our hands are constantly touching, clutching and holding objects – all activities which tense the muscles. Massage is a great way to give them a well-deserved stretch. (And, again, it helps your hands stay limber. If you think of how stiff an old person's hands are, if you've ever watched your granny try to manage a can opener, then you'll understand the value of keeping hands strong and flexible.)

This simple massage takes just five minutes. The terrific bonus is that when you've done it a couple of times and got the hang of the movements, you can do it at the office – it's a brilliant break from working at your screen – waiting for a bus, watching TV, or even in bed...

You don't need to use a special oil – just a squirt of your favourite hand cream is all it takes.

1 After you've applied the cream, breathe in – and as you breathe out, press your thumb into the fleshy part of the opposite hand, between the thumb and forefinger. Squeezing the flesh, move your massaging thumb in small, firm circles over the entire area.

2 Turn your hand over and repeat on the palm. Concentrate on the thick pads of muscle on each side of the hand.

3 Glide the thumb between the knuckles, working up the grooves towards the wrist.

4 Press and hold the side of each finger. Work from base down to tip, pulling each finger towards you, and gently twist each finger at the knuckles. At the tip, squeeze and firmly pull each finger.

9.30 P.M. LOOSEN YOUR TONGUE

The jaw is one of the most stress-prone zones – especially when you have to bite your tongue and bottle up what's really annoying you. Even in your sleep, you can grit your teeth so

If you do this exercise just after brushing your teeth before bedtime, it should keep the jaw beautifully relaxed all night long (no more stressed-out tooth-grinding...)

hard that you wake up aching right across your chin. The quickest way to get relief is to press your tongue lightly to the roof of your mouth, just behind the front teeth, and hold for a count of five. Repeat several times. Then place two fingertips over each jaw hinge (by your earlobes), press in gently, open your mouth and move your jaw from side to side and up and down for a count of thirty. Finally, open your eyes and mouth wide, stick out your tongue as far as possible and hold for a count of twelve – not a pretty sight, but it feels great afterwards! If you do this exercise just after brushing your teeth before bedtime, it should keep the jaw beautifully relaxed all night long. (No more stressed-out tooth-grinding...)

10.00 P.M. MIND/BODY JOURNAL

Review the day's experiences; analyse what you loved about the day – or what made you feel uncomfortable. Writing down your feelings helps you get in touch with them. (We're generally very bad at that!) If you're worried that when your life's revved up again you won't remember your good intentions – to walk more, take an aromatherapy course, have regular skin-clearing facials – write yourself a note to remind yourself what you'd like to try again, or to explore further. And stick it on the fridge …

10.15 P.M. SLEEP...

To sleep, perchance to dream …

CHAPTER EIGHT

Sunday Morning

7.30 A.M. RISE AND SHINE

Sunday mornings should be all about lazing around – and this one is no different. You'll be discovering relaxation techniques that should stay with you for the rest of your life – and simply chilling out, unwinding. (But try to resist the temptation to read the Sunday papers. Give yourself a break from the world's bad news…)

8.00 A.M. SALUTE TO THE SUN

As you did yesterday, begin your day with a cup of herbal tea and the yoga Salute to the Sun, together with the other simple yoga postures you learned yesterday.

9.00 A.M. JUICE MEAL OR WHOLEFOOD BREAKFAST

9.15 A.M. AROMATHERAPY HOT TOWEL FACIAL

As Saturday 9.15 a.m. (see page 63).

10.00 A.M. MORNING WALK

When you get home, put the spring back in your step by massaging your arches – any cylinder will do, such as a cold fizzy drink can, a rolling pin, a frozen can of juice. While seated, put the cylinder on the floor and – pressing firmly – roll your foot back and forth over it for a few minutes until you feel better.

10.45 A.M. LEARN HOW TO BREATHE ...

We all *think* we know how to breathe – after all, we do it day in, day out, every day. But most people breathe shallowly, which can give rise to feelings of anxiety and confusion and make it difficult to focus the mind. If you can shift to deep, rhythmic breathing – even for just a few

> Breath work can help relieve almost any situation involving anxiety, stress or tension: insomnia, public speaking, even asking for a rise

minutes a day, to start with, until it becomes a good-health habit – then you'll almost certainly find it easier to stay on top of things. Breath work can help relieve almost any situation involving anxiety, stress or tension – insomnia, public speaking, even asking for a rise. From a physical point of view, correct breathing is energising and even rejuvenating. When we are deeply relaxed, our breathing becomes deeper and slower. But it works the other way round, too. Breathe more deeply and more slowly, and you can *induce* relaxation ...

One of the best breath techniques is the full yogic breath (which does not have to be performed while performing a headstand, mercifully!). Ideally, you should do this twice a day – first thing, before your 'Salute to the Sun' (see page 57), and again at night, especially if you're feeling stressed-to-excess. It's also ideal if you've got an important date or an important job interview coming up.

- Lie down on the floor, on your back, with your hands slightly away from your body. Palms should face the ceiling, legs should be relaxed and a few inches apart. (You can do this in a chair, in which case you should keep your feet flat on the floor, your shoulders and waist relaxed. This is not a time to start worrying about a Marilyn Monroe pot belly.)

- Move your hands to rest lightly on your lower abdomen. Feel the muscles of the abdomen expand as you inhale and contract as you exhale. Do this for around seven breaths.
- Now move your hands to your lower ribs, at the side. Relax your elbows and shoulders so that you can feel the space in your ribcage. You'll be aware of a feeling of 'openness'. Feel your fingers moving upwards and outwards as the ribcage expands. Do this for around seven breaths, too.
- Place your fingertips on your collarbone and rest them there lightly. As you inhale, be aware of a widening across the collarbone and the expansion across the shoulders. (When you've got the hang of yogic breathing, there's no need to go through the hand motions every time. It's just to increase your awareness of the feelings you should experience when you're doing it properly.)

When you get good at yogic breathing, this entire in-out motion can be completed in one breath, filling first the lower abdomen, then the middle chest, then the upper chest with one steady breath – and then breathe out the opposite way. If you can, relax in a horizontal position for a few moments while your breathing returns to normal, to maximise the benefits. Just five minutes of yogic breathing can change you from a woman-on-the-verge-of-a-nervous-breakdown into an altogether calmer, more serene creature…

11.30 A.M. HERBAL TEATIME

Herbal teas have been enjoyed for their medicinal properties for centuries. A herb is defined as any plant that can be used for

medicinal, aromatic or culinary pur-
poses. All natural food stores offer
shelf upon shelf of pre-packed
herbal teas these days, but you may
find that brewing your own, with
herbs bought from a herbalist – or
better still, plucked from the garden
– is more satisfying. (See Resources
for details of how to mail order
herbs.) Because you're seeking to
de-tox during your spa weekend, you
may want to sip teas and *tisanes* that

> *Because you're
> seeking to de-tox
> during your spa
> weekend, you
> may want to sip
> teas and tisanes
> that specifically
> help elimination*

specifically help elimination. If you're a bit of a caffeine addict,
though, you may experience some unwelcome side-effects.

A little caffeine can be a wonderful thing – it's a jolt to the
system that can get you through tough times and revive you
before an important meeting or date. Unfortunately, many of
us are locked in the caffeine trap: we *need* caffeine to get us
going. We're trapped in a spiral of tiredness: we're exhausted
– so we drink a caffeinated drink. That gives us instant oomph
– but drops us down again, when it wears off, leaving us more
weary than we were before. The only thing that can get us off
this caffeine treadmill is to go 'cold turkey' on caffeine, so
that the body can start to work with its own energy reserves,
rather than relying on that java jolt.

But giving up – depending on the level of your regular
intake – can trigger tiredness and lethargy, snappiness, awe-
some headaches, even the shakes! Nevertheless, a de-toxing
spa weekend *is* the perfect time to try to beat that caffeine
dependency, if it's something you feel you should do: your
diary will be empty, so if you *do* suffer any withdrawal
symptoms, you can have a nap, or otherwise cope with them,

without them interfering with your work. (The commonest side-effect is a crushing headache, more common if you're giving up coffee rather than tea – tea contains a different member of the caffeine family that doesn't trigger the same highs and lows. If you really feel you can't bear it, then a cup of decaffeinated coffee should eliminate the symptoms; even decaf contains a small percentage of caffeine.)

Many people, though, don't experience any withdrawal symptoms. Certainly, it's good to give your system a break from caffeine. So here are some herbal alternatives …

Lemon balm and **vervain** teas are especially effective in lifting gloom and depression. If you ever feel depressed, try an infusion of lemon balm three times a day for a month; it works wonders. (If you do have a tendency to depression, it's particularly important to quit caffeine-drinking, which only exacerbates the fatigue which is characteristic of depression. Instead of coffee, try **rosemary** tea – it really perks you up.)

Peppermint tea is a terrific pick-me-up if you feel weary.

Rosehip tea is a great stress-buster.

Take **feverfew** tea if you're suffering from a headache.

If you suffer from fluctuating hormones (the menopause, or premenstrual syndrome), then drink **sage** tea whenever you feel like it.

If you feel bloated, do a bit of weeding! Excellent teas for purifying the bloodstream can be brewed from **nettles, dandelion root, cleavers** (a.k.a. **goose grass**), **burdock** or **echinacea**.

Dandelion is also good for getting rid of cellulite; its diuretic effect helps speed up the elimination of toxins – through the increased rate of urination it promotes. (You can also buy delicious, roasted dandelion 'coffee' in good health food stores.) If you suffer from lots of colds and flu, take a cup of **echinacea** tea once a day. (This extraordinary herb actually makes your mouth tingle as you drink it – so you feel it *must* be doing something!)

At night, make a healing tea of **cinnamon** (infuse the bark); add milk or soya milk and a touch of honey to send you off to a blissful night's sleep.

If you suffer from sleeplessness, **chamomile** is the traditional tea-of-choice – but **catnip** is another tranquilliser.

Limeflower tea is also good for insomniacs, as is **orange blossom** tea (widely available in tea bags). **Valerian** tea is another useful sedative, great before bedtime.

11.45 A.M. LEARN TO BE HERE NOW...

How much of your day do you spend living in 'present time'? Most of us have an ever-present sensation that life is rushing by (and leaving us behind!). But part of the problem is that we tend to spend our time thinking about what we're going to be doing/saying later. In other words, your body may be eating a tuna sandwich – but your mind is fast-forwarding to what you're going to say in your afternoon meeting.

There are simple ways to get your mind back 'in the moment' – and your home spa weekend is the perfect time to get in the habit. (And it is a habit: the

The more you practice, the easier you'll find it to 'be here now' – rather than to wish your life away

more you practice, the easier you'll find it to 'be here now' – rather than to wish your life away.)

According to Gloria Keeling, founder of the Mind–Body Fitness Institute in Maui, Hawaii, these simple exercises will help you experience life to the maximum – and make the most of 'present time'.

So ...

- At least once a day while you're eating, eat very slowly and savour each bite. Pay attention to the taste and texture of your food.
- While you're out walking, count your breaths with each step. Be aware of how quickly or slowly you are breathing. When you encounter a stressful moment, notice your breathing. Take slower, deeper breaths to feel more calm.
- Find five minutes and allow yourself to be utterly, completely, absolutely still. (You can use this time to meditate if you like.)
- Whenever you're exercising, try not to think about what you're going to have for dinner or what your friend told you on the phone. Instead, just think about how your body is feeling as it moves.
- You may have chosen to spend this weekend in a solitary 'retreat', away from the outside world. But if you're sharing your home spa with a friend or partner, make the effort to *concentrate* on what they're really saying. (It's the biggest compliment you can pay someone.) Try not to think about how you will respond to them, let alone interrupt; instead, focus all your attention on listening well.

CHAPTER NINE

Sunday Afternoon

12.00 NOON JUICE MEAL OR WHOLEFOOD LUNCH

1.00 P.M. BODY BRUSHING BLITZ

The action of gentle skin brushing stimulates circulation and whisks dead cells from the surface of your skin, leaving it gleaming and glowing. (Supermodels *swear* by skin brushing.) Skin-brushing is also a valuable part of any anti-cellulite programme – one of the few things that really *works*.

> *Skin-brushing is also a valuable part of any anti-cellulite programme – one of the few things that really* works

What you'll need:

• A natural bristle body brush, a loofah or a scrub mitt

Always brush with gentle strokes, beginning with the soles of the feet, then moving up your legs, hips and abdomen. Move on to your arms, from fingertips to shoulders, across your torso (avoiding the nipples!) and back, finishing with your neck. In an ideal world, you'd skin-brush every day. It's perfect before any beauty treatment, or a pampering bath. Try to make skin-brushing part of your life. Your whole system will love you for it.

1.30 P.M. D-I-Y HYDROTHERAPY

This is the kind of thing that people check into £1,000-a-week spas to enjoy.

Hydrotherapy literally means 'water healing' and was introduced by a Dominican monk from Bavaria called Sebastian

Kneipp (1821–1897). It's a popular form of treatment using hot and cold water to boost circulation, ease aches and stiffness and deep-cleanse the skin. Modern shower heads can easily be adapted for home hydrotherapy as long as the temperature can be changed from hot to cold very quickly.

To make the most of hydrotherapy, you should alternate the shower temperature. Start on a gentle, warm heat, then get gradually hotter over one or two minutes. Flick to cold for 15 seconds, then back to hot and then cold for as long as you can bear, ending with up to 5 minutes at neutral, body temperature. As hot water is more cleansing, take the opportunity of the hot-water bursts to brush vigorously or use a scrub, always working towards the heart, and making sure you follow with that cool blast of water to help circulation and skin tone.

Remember, when you are back to the hurly burly of life, that hot showers can be tiring as well as relaxing, so limit them to five-minute bursts.

2.00 P.M. CATCH UP WITH YOUR LIFE

Spa weekends are about getting back in touch with ourselves, skipping a beat, re-prioritising in a frantic world. Do you have a guilt-inducing pile of correspondence that you never seem to get round to answering: not bills (they're banned, for the weekend at least), but letters from old friends, changes of address, birth announcements, invitations that you *meant* to respond to – before life got in the way? (I do.) In advance of your spa weekend, buy yourself a stack of art postcards – perhaps from a museum store or a gallery. Make a point of seeking out the most beautiful, inspiring cards you can find; they give enormous pleasure to whoever's on the receiving end – especially when they're out of the blue! (If you don't think you can bear to part with them, buy two copies of favourite images – one for yourself.) Find a real fountain pen, not a Biro, then sit down – preferably at a table in front of a window – and write to everyone you've been *meaning* to write to. Experience the *pleasure* of unhurried writing. (It's amazing how quickly your handwriting improves when you're not stressed.) Soon, you'll have a small stack of pretty cards, ready for stamping – and will have assuaged a huge amount of guilt.

3.00 P.M. GET FIT – WITH A TWIST

For most of us, our waists (if we can find them!) are a problem zone, the place where fat tends to accumulate first. But

> *For a sleeker middle, try belly dancing!*

one of the reasons we bulge in the middle is because we don't exercise those muscles. (A desk-bound life is the enemy of an hourglass waist.) So, for a sleeker middle, try belly dancing! Surprisingly, this ancient art is also a modern shape-up.

Centuries ago, when belly dancing was first practised in the Middle East, its serpentine moves were meant for an eminently practical purpose – to attract a husband. Today, although the seductive body language survives, this ritual is taking on a whole new role (roll?): these undulations and gestures are being used to firm up womanly curves, with the advantage that the no-stress twists are gentle on muscles and joints. Unlike aerobics, the moves are natural to the human body – and intended to work the entire body at once, rather than develop it bit by bit. (Unlike, say, weight training.) They are also terrific fun (and will probably give you the best giggle of the weekend).

The circle Stand with feet a few inches apart and knees relaxed. Rotate hips, as if your hipbones are following a hula-hoop.

The roll With feet apart and knees relaxed, swing the right hip up and to the right side, raising your right heel off the floor simultaneously. Then swing to the left, raising that hip and heel. Each side of your pelvis will follow the outline of a half-circle.

The undulating arch Begin in starting position, feet a few inches apart and knees relaxed. Lift ribcage and stick your chest out slightly in front of the rest of your body. Holding this position, lean the upper body back, tilting the pelvis forwards, with knees very bent. Then, pulling the abdominals in, round your shoulders and straighten the legs. Slowly extend the spine and return to the starting position. (If this sounds complicated, just think: undulation!)

If you really enjoy yourself, you might want to pursue belly dancing further by signing up for a class, which really is fantastic exercise for your middle and hips. Look under 'Dance' in the Yellow Pages; many dance studios and even local authorities offer belly dancing classes.

3.15 P.M. DE-JUNK YOUR BATHROOM CABINET

Housework is banned during your spa weekend, except for a little washing-up, if necessary. Even if you have a dishwasher, it's best not to switch it on. Our lives are dominated by noise, which impacts on our lives and stresses us even without us realising. Aim to have a machine-free weekend.

De-junking your make-up bag and bathroom cabinet *isn't* housework, though; it's good for the soul – and streamlines your regime, for the future, saving you time (and probably money). Most of us have *way* too much beauty 'stuff'. (As you will have begun to understand, during your spa weekend, some highly effective cosmetics can be made fresh from your fridge, rather than paid for in department stores. In future, you might want to haunt your local greengrocer – rather than the marbled beauty halls – in your quest for interesting new cosmetics!)

What many people are belatedly discovering is – as *Absolutely Fabulous* actress Joanna Lumley points out – 'Things don't bring you happiness. But perhaps you only acquire that wisdom as you get older. So we go through life longing to acquire things – a new freezer, a new dress, a lipstick, anything you think is magically going to transform your life. Then

> **What most of us crave, fundamentally, is more time**

you get it, the money's gone – and you feel worse than you did before.' What most of us crave, fundamentally, is more time. So if you can *save* time, on a daily basis, not rummaging around in the bottom of your make-up bag or in your dressing room drawer – looking for that foundation/lipstick/moisturiser you *know* you put somewhere – then that's a valuable gift.

Medicine cabinets and dressing tables can be virtual museums of packaging/bottles/pots. Which is fine if you've set your heart on collecting vintage scent bottles – but tends, instead, to arise from misplaced guilt at getting rid of an expensive beauty treat or vitamin store indulgence. (Even if it brought you out in a rash.) Here are suggestions for an hour spent 'space clearing' (as

New Age gurus call de-junking) your bathroom cabinet, make-up bag and medicine shelf. I promise, you'll feel wonderfully purged!

- Throw out every half-finished prescription cream or pill, which not only take up space but could be downright dangerous if you opt to 'self-prescribe' in future. Return left-over medicine and tablets to doctors' surgeries for safe disposal.
- Empty medicine bottles are refillable – take them back.
- The potency of vitamins is reduced over time, too. You are better off eating a fresh orange than a three-year-old vitamin C tablet.
- Bin last summer's suncare preparations. Overwintering them in the bathroom cabinet may reduce their SPF power, so exposing you to sunburn next summer.
- Don't hang on to outer packaging, or (once you've read them) those flimsy little origami-ed instruction sheets. Remember: they can usually be recycled with the newspapers.
- Nobody needs that many lipsticks. One top make-up artist (who shall remain nameless) has a theory that any two lipstick colours mixed together look good.
- If that's too radical, you can simplify life by achieving several different finishes from a single shade – once you know how. (Spend a few minutes in front of the mirror, practising. Keep make-up remover on hand, to swipe away lipstick after you've experimented.)

For sheer cover, outline the lips with the edge of the lipstick, then cover the entire lip with colourless gloss (or lip salve), and gently rub the lips together.

For high gloss, put on lipstick as you normally would, then coat with a clear gloss.

For semi-matte colour, put a tissue between your lips and gently blot, to take away shine.

For intense colour, wear a deep shade alone.

For shimmer, apply lipstick lightly, then cover with a sweep of an old pearlised lipstick.

- Don't double up on beauty products if you don't have to: hair conditioner or hand lotion works on legs as shaving cream – leaving skin ultra-silky.
- Aluminium containers for beauty products – now favoured by everyone from Nicky Clarke to Aveda – can be recycled along with drinks cans at your nearest recycling bank.
- Get rid of every cosmetic beyond its safe shelf-life. That means: three to six months for mascara and liquid eyeliner, up to a year for eye cream and nail varnish, two to three years for moisturiser. Your nose will tell you whether your scent's still wearable – but if you've been keeping it on your dressing table in direct sunlight, it will have gone off. Only keep the empty bottle if you really, truly love it.

> *Offer anything that didn't work for you to friends, to see if it works better for them*

- Most of us spend a fortune searching for the perfect moisturiser – leaving half-used tubs on the bathroom shelf, where they're at-a-glance guilt-triggers. Offer anything which didn't work for you to friends, to see if it works better for them. (But not if they go back longer than a year; throw them out.)
- Donate old lipsticks and blushers to a friend who has small daughters, to put in their 'dressing-up box'. She will be grateful that they won't be raiding *her* make-up bag in future.
- If you truly insist on hanging on to all those bits of old make-up, at least divide them up into useful kits that you can leave everywhere you might need one – the car, your office drawer, the gym.
- You don't need containers of air freshener. That's why windows and fans were invented.

- Discipline yourself. Make a vow not to treat yourself to a new body lotion till you're down to the last drops of the one you're using now. Or you never *will* finish this one, and it'll just hang around gathering dust. (Likewise eye-make-up removers, cleansers, moisturisers.)

4.00 P.M. AFTERNOON WALK

5.00 P.M. IT'S A WRAP

Your reward for cosmetic de-junking: a blissful 'wrap' treatment. You can make like a mermaid – or wallow in mud. (Only do *one* of these treatments, however. They're effective de-toxers and skin-buffers, and indulging in both, in the space of a single weekend, is overkill – not just for your skin, but for your whole system.)

MARINE MAGIC

What you'll need:

- Seaweed mask (home-made or store-bought)
- Clingfilm or a 'space' blanket from a mountaineering/hiking store
- Large and small towels
- A small pillow
- Larger pillows – the foam kind used on outdoor furniture (or a foam mattress, if you have one)

You may like to steer clear of seaweed at the beach, but this magical marine ingredient offers fabulous benefits for skin. A miracle of the sea – long used as a thickening agent in everything from ice cream to hand cream – seaweed is now taking an active role in a variety of skin-care products. Its fans say that seaweed – actually a generic term for more than 20,000 species of algae that grow in the world's oceans – can do no wrong. It moisturises,

You may like to steer clear of seaweed at the beach, but this magical marine ingredient offers fabulous benefits for skin

yet controls too. It counteracts the ageing effects of pollution on the skin. Historically, seaweed's been used in fascinating, skin-saving ways. According to Miriam Polne-Fuller, PhD, a research biologist at the University of California in Santa Barbara, primitive people used seaweed paste to treat burns because 'it's soothing and inhibits bacterial infections'.

Europe's 18th- and 19th-century aristocracy used seaweed and seawaters as a general cure-all. Today, Lydia Sarfati, president and founder of US beauty company Repêchage – one of the first American companies to borrow from Europe the concept of seaweed as a beauty treat – relies on the plant in her treatments because 'seaweed provides all the elements needed for proper functioning of healthy skin'. One of seaweed's main elements, alginic acid, has the ability to bind with harmful waste products in our body, aiding their elimination from our system. The Japanese long ago recognised the energising potential of seaweed, with its high level of the vital-for-life mineral iodine, which has a regulating effect on the body's metabolism. What is now being recognised is that an algae body masque or algae-rich soak actually remineralises from the outside in.

Algae wraps are becoming popular salon beauty treatments. But it's now possible to buy seaweed-based 'sludge' for an at-home wrap or body mask. Brands based on seaweed include Thalgo, Thalacap, Repêchage and Phytomer, while

E'SPA (the aromatherapy-based company) also produce a delicious seaweed-based product for treatments at home. (For mail-order details of these sea-based ranges, see Resources.)

Alternatively – and less expensively – if you live anywhere near a seaweedy beach and you own a blender or a food processor, you can harvest your own and concoct a fresh seaweed wrap! Any seaweed will do, but before use, make sure to wash the seaweed in fresh-running water to remove any sand particles and pollutants. Then, if you have a blender or a food processor, put small amounts of seaweed in this and whizz it up with two tablespoonfuls of any of the oils which are particularly compatible with skin: jojoba oil, grapeseed oil, wheatgerm oil or almond oil, which are widely available in natural food stores; try to buy the organic versions, where possible. (Warning: don't put too much at once in the blender; some seaweeds can be quite hard to chop.) You can then apply the sludge to your skin, as you'll see.

Note Seaweed treatments are de-toxifying, stimulating, re-mineralising and deep cleansing. Seaweed and sea water treatments shouldn't be enjoyed late at night, because the iodine – which is essential for metabolic functioning – can be absorbed through the skin, keeping you wide-awake!

Bathing in seaweed – if you'd like to try it simply add fronds of seaweed to your bathwater, or use a commercially prepared product such as E'SPA's De-toxifying Seaweed Bath (see Resources) – is thought to alleviate a host of minor ailments from period pains to muscular tension. Again, the optimum time to make like a mermaid is during the day – unless you want to toss and turn all night...

For perfect at-home wraps, it's best to get hold of a mountaineer's 'space' blanket, a hypothermia-defying silver sheet made of a fabric called Mylar in which climbers wrap themselves to beat the cold. If you wrap yourself in one at home, your body heat is also trapped within the blanket, turbo-charging the treatment as you warm up.

Once you've made up your paste – it's best used fresh – or slathered on the branded seaweed mixture, it's time to cocoon yourself, lie back and let the oligo-elements de-tox and cleanse you. Most of us don't have the luxury of a massage table at home (in a salon, you'll have your seaweed wrap on a comfortable table). However, it's possible to improvise, on the floor in your bathroom. In order to pad this and make it comfy and more welcoming than bare tiles, you'll need a stack of towels, a small pillow or cushion and some larger cushions (preferably the thin, foam kind you use on garden furniture), plus a large blanket. So before you start your wrap, lay the cushions on the floor, and cover with the largest bath towel you have. Wrap the small pillow in another towel and lay it at the head of the other cushions. If you have a space blanket, lay this on the towels.

Now you are ready to slather on your seaweed paste/mask, whether home-made or store-bought. You can apply it all over your body, or you can spot-target trouble spots – for instance, your legs or upper arms, or your tummy area. (Some therapists avoid using it on the breasts.) Once you have slathered on the seaweed mixture, wrap the area round and round in clingfilm, which serves a dual purpose: it prevents sludge from getting all over your towels, and again, it encourages the skin to warm up, for maximum absorption of the vital oligo-elements present in seaweed. Then wrap yourself in the silver blanket, leaving your hands free so that you can pull the larger blanket over your body, on top of everything, to make you even warmer. You'll become toasty in no time.

Don't cover your face – you need to breathe! The Mylar

blanket should keep you warm enough to sweat the toxins out of your skin, without making you too uncomfortable. If you feel a little cool, pull up a blanket. If you feel too hot, loosen the blanket a bit.

After 20 minutes, unwrap yourself, shower off any remaining seaweed, pat skin dry and slather on moisturiser.

WALLOW IN MUD

An alternative to the seaweed wrap is a mud treatment. Mud, like seaweed, is intensely rich in minerals, which can be absorbed through the skin to revive and restore. At the same time, the mud – or clay – draws impurities to the surface of the skin which are

> *Mud – or clay – draws impurities to the surface of the skin which are literally sluiced down the plug-hole after your treatment*

literally sluiced down the plug-hole after your treatment. (Clay treatments are particularly good, then, for oily or blemished skins.)

Clay comes in a number of colours, depending on its mineral content. Green clay is the most widely used, and is recognised as the most powerfully therapeutic. Red clay is a useful tonic for convalescence and because of its iron content, good for anaemia and fatigue. White clay – a.k.a. kaolinite – is milder in action, making it suitable even for babies and sensitive skins. Yellow clay is often prescribed for joint and skin problems, and for exhaustion, while pink clay – actually a mixture of red and white – is popular as a mask for tired, dry or ultra-sensitive skins.

Clays and muds can be found at good health food stores (or by mail order – see Resources), but one of the best pre-mixed commercially prepared products is Princess Marcella Borghese's

Fango/Active Mud, featuring essential-oil-scented mud from Italy's Montecatini natural spa-for-the-rich. Fango/Active Mud is a volcanic sludge that de-toxifies and deliciously remineralises body skin in a hippo-ish 10-minute treatment that positively *demands* you stay relaxed and immobile – unless you're prepared to sluice down the muddy prints from your *boudoir* afterwards!

Mix your chosen mud according to instructions, slather it on, then wrap yourself in the 'space blanket', and lie down on the floor and relax. If you find the clay gets uncomfortably tight and taut, spritz it with a plant mister to prevent it drying out. When fifteen minutes are up, follow the instructions as for the seaweed wrap, sluicing away every last trace of mud with cool water, reach for a sponge, if you find it hard to rinse off. (Don't be tempted to scrub off the mud.)

Yet another alternative to a mud wrap is a mud *bath*. One of the most famous sources of therapeutic mud is the Neydharting Moor, about 60 km from Salzburg in Austria. Known as 'Moor' or 'Moor-Life', the mud has been investigated and analysed by over 500 scientists and has been found to be unique. Because the 20,000-year-old glacial valley basin in which it lies was first a lake and then a moor, where the waters have never drained away, it's retained all of its organic, mineral and trace elements. (It's available in health food stores, or by mail order – see Resources.)

Simply add two-thirds of a cup of Moor Bath to warm water for an instantly relaxing treatment – and don't be put off by the fact that the water turns black; the results are blissful! Relax in the water for 20 minutes, then wrap yourself in a warm towel and rest for at least half an hour. (For a therapeutic course, it's recommended to continue the treatment with a mud bath every other day for three weeks.)

You can turbo-charge the de-toxifying effects of the bath by sipping a cup of cleansing herbal tea: look for teas that contain burdock, dandelion, red clover, nettles, sarsaparilla or yarrow. These herbs gently de-toxify the body by stimulating the eliminative functions of the skin, liver, kidneys and intestines, helping to purify your whole system.

6.00 P.M. FIVE SIMPLE STRETCHES

Our sedentary lives make us stiff. Then when we exercise, or garden, or over-exert ourselves, that makes us stiff, too. Simply stretching helps keeps the body fit and healthy. If you stay limber and 'bendy' into old age, you are statistically less likely to have falls – and the good news is: it's never too late to start to loosen up. Stretching is crucial before and after exercise, too – even walking. If you stretch before you walk, it literally puts more spring into your step and makes it feel effortless. If you stretch *after* you walk, it helps prevent the muscles seizing up.

Here are five simple stretches which should help bring back suppleness. Take each stretch as far as you comfortably can: you should feel a *gentle* tension in the muscle – nothing more. Then hold your position for 20 seconds. After you've done all five stretches once, go back and do them again. You'll almost certainly find that you can stretch further than before. Again, try to make stretching into a daily habit – like brushing your teeth and your hair.

Back stretch Sit all the way back in a sturdy chair which enables your feet to touch the floor. Keep them flat on the floor, knees together. Allowing your head to hang down, press your chest on to your thighs and lightly grip the front legs of the chair with your hands. Relax your shoulders and pull gently downwards with your arms. Hold for 20 seconds.

Torso stretch Slowly lift your torso back to an upright position. Lengthen your neck and sit up tall. Keeping your hips facing forwards, gently twist to your left from the waist and grasp the back of your chair with both hands. Turn your head to the left and look behind you. Pull very gently with your left arm, but take care not to tense your shoulders or neck. You should feel the stretch along both sides. Make sure to keep both thighs on the chair. Hold. Switch directions, then repeat.

Back of thigh stretch Still sitting in the chair, face forward. Straighten and lift your left leg as high as you comfortably can, without rounding your back. Contract your lower abdominal muscle and, keeping your shoulders relaxed, grasp your left leg under your thigh with one hand and hold on to your calf with your other hand. (Bend your left knee slightly if this position isn't comfortable.) If you use your strong hand (right hand if you're right-handed) on your calf, you'll get better leverage. But be gentle! *Gently* pull your left leg towards your torso, while keeping your back as upright and straight as possible. Hold. Switch legs and repeat.

Calf stretch Stand and face the seat of the chair, about two feet away from it, knees slightly bent. Bending at the hips, grasp the sides of the seat with both hands. Keeping your back flat and head in line with your spine, bend your left knee and step back with your right foot until your back is parallel with the floor. If you don't feel the stretch in your right calf, step back further with your right foot. Hold. Switch legs and repeat. (This is an excellent stretch for before and after walking – and you don't even need a chair. Simply stand in front of a wall and bend your arms, putting your palms flat on the wall, shoulder width apart. Bending one knee, step back with the other leg until you feel the stretch. Hold for 20 seconds on each leg, then repeat at least once.)

Neck and shoulder stretch Stand with your feet shoulder width apart, knees slightly bent, abdominal muscles tight, chest open, shoulders relaxed and head in line with your spine. Reach behind you with both hands and grasp your right wrist with your left hand. Gently pull your right arm downwards to lengthen your right shoulder. Tilt your head towards your left shoulder to stretch the right side of your neck. Hold. Switch sides, then repeat.

CHAPTER TEN

Sunday Evening

6.30 P.M. EVENING MEDITATION

Continue the practice you started yesterday.

7.00 P.M. JUICE MEAL OR WHOLEFOOD SUPPER

8.00 P.M. D-I-Y FACIAL MASSAGE

By now, you should be utterly relaxed and free of headaches, tension or anxiety. But it's still a good time to learn facial massage techniques which can help banish aches, pains, cares and woes – and will unwind you beautifully for another night of restful sleep.

Learn facial massage techniques which can help banish aches, pains, cares and woes

1 Rest your elbows on a table – or your dressing table. Lower your head into your hands until your eyes are resting on the heel of your hands. Hold for 30 seconds, then move your hands to your eyebrows and glide them across your brows towards your temples. Work up the forehead with movements like this until you reach the hairline.
2 Rest your fingers on your temples, releasing your neck as much as possible so that your fingers are almost holding your head up. On breathing out, rotate your fingers slowly clockwise.
3 Place the balls of your thumbs underneath the inner edge of

your eyebrows. (This can be a little tender, so be conscious that that's normal.) Hold the pressure for ten seconds, release – then repeat. Work along the browbone towards the temples.

4 Place the balls of your thumbs under your cheekbones, resting the weight of your head and neck on your thumbs. Breathe out and glide your thumbs across the cheekbones towards your ears.

5 Position your fingertips along your upper lip and press firmly into the gums.

6 Take hold of your jawbone at your chin, between your fingers and thumbs. Press firmly into the jaw and as you breathe out, slowly rotate the fingers into the bone. Move the fingers and thumbs along and work outwards towards your ears.

7 Lift your elbows off the table and place your fingers at the top of your neck, behind the ears, leaning forwards slightly. Breathe out, and while you're exhaling, lean the pads of your fingers into the base of your skull, and rotate slowly. Work slowly inwards, and then downwards to the bottom of the neck. (Don't do this movement if you have neck problems without consulting a health practitioner first.)

8 Supporting one arm on the other, bring your free hand up to massage the opposite shoulder. Tilt your head to one side, starting from the neck, squeeze the muscle slowly and deeply between the heel of your hand and your fingers. Continue right out to the shoulder joint (and even the upper arms). Repeat twice.

9 In the same position, place the pads of your fingers on top of the muscle that lies below your collarbone, just slightly lower down your chest. (You'll feel the bulge slightly.) As you breathe out, press your fingers into the muscle and rotate slowly, working across the top of the muscle. Repeat twice.

10 Rest your elbows on the table again. Place the heels of your hands just in front of the hairline on your forehead and allow the full weight of your neck and head to rest on your hands. As you breathe out, slowly rotate the heels of your hands. Work over the front, sides and back of the head. To finish, slide your fingers into your (gleaming, beautifully conditioned!) hair – and comb them through from the roots to the ends. Work thoroughly through the hair, one hand after another.

8.30 P.M. AQUACADABRA

Before bed, treat yourself to another sleep-inducing aromatherapy bath. (See pages 44 to 47 for some essential oil combinations.)

9.00 P.M. THE PERFECT 10 (FINGERNAILS, THAT IS...)

On almost every New York street corner, you'll find a manicurist: having a weekly manicure costs around $10 and is a groomed woman's must. But elsewhere, salon visits are expensive – and time-consuming –

With a little practice, you can learn to do a salon-perfect manicure at home

so the good news is that, with a little practice, you can learn to do a salon-perfect manicure at home. However, don't make this a one-off: nails (like cats and small children) respond gratefully to short bursts of attention! If you lavish attention on them, little and often, they will reward you by looking beautiful – and the bonus is, you'll swiftly boost nail health. (Gentle nail-buffing, for instance – with a special nail buffer, which you'll find in pharmacies and beauty halls – improves circulation to the nail bed, improving growth and strength.) In addition, if you suffer from poor nail quality – flaking, breaking, splitting – try eating foods rich in iron, zinc, selenium and vitamin C. Good sources are fruits, green vegetables (including broccoli, Brussels sprouts, cauliflower), potatoes and rosehips.

1 Remove nail polish using a cotton pad and a cuticle stick which has been wrapped, candy-floss-style, in cotton wool. (Warning: never use a wooden or metal instrument on your nails unless it's been carefully buffered with cotton wool first.) Ask at your usual beauty supply store or pharmacy for acetone-free polish remover, if possible, as others can lead to cracking; alternatively, look for the words 'gentle' or 'non-drying' on the label, which are clues.

2 Shorten any nails that need cutting down – using nail scissors in preference to clippers, as these can cause cracks. Cut from the side to the middle of the nail, then shape the nails with an emery board, stroking lightly from the edges of the nail towards the centre. (The softer and springier the board, the better. Look for the new kinds which are almost squishy to the touch, thanks to their foam backing.)

3 Apply a cuticle cream to soften the cuticle. A cuticle oil – usually containing almond oil – is perfect, but baby oil works well, too. Massage it in with circular movements of the thumb.

4 Soak fingertips in a bowl of warm, soapy water for at least a minute and dry thoroughly afterwards.

5 Gently push back the skin around the cuticles, working away dead tissue to create a neat, clean line. (Again, use a cuticle stick wrapped in cotton wool, or better still, a special rubber-tipped 'hoof stick', which you can get from beauty supply stores and pharmacies.) Cuticles are important because they protect the base of the growing nail, so it's vital not to abuse them.

6 Wash hands thoroughly and brush nails with a soft nail brush. Rinse the nails and dry them carefully on a towel. (Even a tiny amount of moisture or oil will spoil your manicure by preventing the polish from adhering to the nail.)

7 Brush on a protective base coat to cover the entire nail surface, stopping short of the cuticle. A base coat will also stop polish staining nails.

8 Apply two coats of your chosen nail colour, starting with a stroke down the centre of the nail and then a stroke either side, being careful to avoid the cuticle. (If you do smudge the polish, dip an orange stick in remover and carefully wipe the smudge away.) Be careful not to overload the brush with polish to ensure even application (and swifter drying); two thin coats are better than one thick coat. (What colour nail polish will you choose? Slim, elegant fingers look good with any shade. But if your hands aren't your most attractive feature, avoid using bright colours that will draw attention to them and stick to the more natural-looking colours, instead.)

9 Lightly brush on one layer of top coat to add gloss and protect against chipping and abrasion. (To prolong the life of your manicure, brush on a fresh layer of top coat every other day.)

10 Ideally, you should allow your nails half-an-hour to be completely dry. There's a world of difference between 'touch-dry' and hard, and a smudge on an otherwise perfect set of nails is really irritating. So allow yourself thirty minutes of pure relaxation. (And try to sleep with hands outside the sheets, to prevent imprints!)

10.00 P.M. MIND/BODY JOURNAL

Take this, the last day of the spa, to reflect on what you've learned from writing about your experiences. And consider how valuable it will be to 'keep up the good work'. It isn't always easy to carve an entire weekend out of your schedule for a health spa at home – but you don't *have* to; once a week or once a month, set aside an evening to indulge yourself. When time is tight between home spa sessions, use the quickest treatments in this book to boost your mind – and revitalise your body.

10.15 P.M. SLEEP...

RESOURCES

AROMATHERAPY

If you're interested in finding out more about aromatherapy,
or locating a practitioner near you, send an A5 s.a.e. to:
The Secretary, Aromatherapy Organisations Council,
3 Latymer Close, Braybrooke, Market Harborough,
Leicestershire LE16 8LN. Tel/fax: 01858 434242

BACH FLOWER REMEDIES

For a list of practitioners or details of stockists, write to:
Dr Edward Bach Centre, Mount Vernon, Sotwell, Wallingford,
Oxfordshire OX10 0PZ. Tel: 01491 834678

MASSAGE

For details of courses offered by the London College
of Massage, or to find out more about massage treatment,
contact them at:.
London College of Massage, 5–6 Newman Passage,
London W1P 3PF. Tel: 0171 323 3574

MEDITATION

For details of your nearest Transcendental Meditation
teaching centre and a free information pack, tel: 0990 143733

REFLEXOLOGY

To find a reflexologist near you, contact:
The British Reflexology Association, Monks Orchard,
Whitbourne, Worcestershire WR6 5RB. Tel: 018868 21207

YOGA

For a list of yoga practitioners, send an A5 s.a.e. to:
The British Wheel of Yoga, 1 Hamilton Place, Boston Road,
Sleaford, Lincolnshire NG34 7ES. Tel: 01529 306851

AROMATHERAPY AT HOME

The following companies make wonderful pre-mixed massage blends. Contact them for stockists and/or mail order.

Aesop
Harrods will mail order this range anywhere in the world. Call them
on: 0800 375 1234 (or 44 171 730 1234 from outside the UK).

Elemis
At beauty salons throughout the UK. For details and mail
order, contact: 57–65 The Broadway, Stanmore,
Middlesex HA7 4DU. Tel: 0181 954 8033

E'SPA
This is now available in more than 200 outlets around the
UK. For details of your nearest stockist and for mail order,
telephone their hotline: 01483 454444.

HERBAL TEAS

Neal's Yard (see Cosmetics at Home, overleaf) supply herbs
for making your own teas.
Hambleden Herbs is another mail-order source of pre-
blended organic herb teas or loose herbs for tea-making.
For a catalogue, call: 01823 401205.

COSMETICS AT HOME

Neal's Yard supply all of the herbs and other ingredients (glycerine, beeswax, essential oils, rosewater and so on) – other than the fresh fruit and vegetables – that you need for making cosmetics at home. For your nearest stockist, call: 0171 498 1686

For mail order, write to or telephone:
Neal's Yard, 31 Kings Street, Manchester M2 6AA.
Tel: 0161 831 7875

SEAWEED/MUD

The following companies make products suitable for at-home wraps and mud baths

Argiletz make clay products specially purified for body treatments (including powders, pastes, soap, toothpaste and shampoo). For further details and information, contact:
Argiletz, Sunny Clay, PO Box 3007, London NW3 2UZ.
Tel: 0171 586 3412/Fax: 0171 586 7892

E'SPA (see page 135) make seaweed products (which can also be slapped on to the body), and a wonderful scalp mud.

Molton Brown offer Sea Moss Bath Salts which are rich in marine elements. For mail order, contact:
Molton Brown By Mail, PO Box 2514, London NW6 1SR.
Tel: 0171 625 6550

Moor Mud is available from Austrian Moor Products Ltd, White Ladies, Maresfield, East Sussex TN22 2HH. Tel: 01825 762658

Repêchage is a New York salon whose seaweed products are now distributed around the world. For your nearest salon selling the range, write/tel:
Repêchage, 5 Hugh Business Park, Bacup Road, Waterfoot, Rossendale, Lancashire BB4 7BX. Tel: 01706 211058

The Clay Company
For the Clay Company's mail-order catalogue of mud wraps and baths for home use, send an s.a.e. to them at:
The Clay Company, Penny Lane, Liverpool L18 1DG

SPONGES

Aveda produce a synthetic body 'sponge' which feels just like the real thing but isn't harvested from the wild, so it's more ecologically sound. For mail order and stockists, call: 0171 410 1600

SPACE BLANKET

These are also known as mountain blankets and are used for keeping climbers and mountaineers warm (as well as for keeping the heat in when you are having a home-based wrap). Find them at youth hostelling and mountaineering supply stores.

WATER FILTERS

BritaWater Filters are available from most branches of Boots, or call Customer Services for your nearest stockist: 01932 770599

BOOKSHELF

The at-home spa weekend, as I've explained, is a 'sampler' of different alternative treatments and indulgences. If you want to find out more about what you've tried this weekend, here's my suggested reading list:

Juice High, Leslie Kenton and Russell Cronin (Ebury Press 1996)
Juicing For Health, Caroline Wheater (Thorsons 1993)
The Complete Book of Massage, Clare Maxwell-Hudson (Dorling Kindersley 1998)
The Massage Book, George Downing (Penguin 1996)
Classic Yoga, Vimla Lalvani (Hamlyn 1996)
Eva Fraser's Face and Body Programme, Eva Fraser (Viking 1998)
Eva Fraser's Facial Workout, Eva Fraser (Viking 1998)